Up the Hill

Up the Hill
FOLK TALES FROM THE GRAVE

James Calvin Schaap

DORDT COLLEGE PRESS

Cover and layout: Rob Haan
All of the photographs: J. C. Schaap

The first edition of this book (2014) was an eBook (eISBN: 978-0-89823-325-4) edited by Ryan C. Christiansen and produced by New Rivers Press c/o MSUM, 1104 7th Avenue South Moorhead, MN 56563
www.newriverspress.com

Copyright © 2016 by James C. Schaap

Fragmentary portions of this book may be freely used by those who are interested in sharing the author's story, insights and observations, so long as the material is not pirated for monetary gain and so long as proper credit is visibly given to the publisher and the author. Others, and those who wish to use larger sections of text, must seek written permission from the publisher.

Printed in the United States of America.

Dordt College Press   www.dordt.edu/DCPcatalog
498 Fourth Avenue NE
Sioux Center, Iowa 51250

ISBN: 978-1-940567-15-0

The Library of Congress Cataloging-in-Publication Data is on file with the Library of Congress, Washington, D.C.
Library of Congress Control Number: 2016936857

All characters appearing in this work are fictitious. Any resemblance to real persons, living or dead, is purely coincidental.

Acknowledgments
"January Thaw," "Where the Tree Falls," and "Unveiled," originally appeared in *Perspectives*. A portion of "Deliverance" originally appeared in *Pro Rege*.

To Harold Aardema (1929-2009)
and Frederick Manfred (1912-1994),
both of whom are here,
up the hill.

Folk Tales from the Grave

Up the Hill 1
The Unveiled 15
The Music of the Spheres 27
Phoenix 41
January Thaw 53
Where the Tree Falls 65
Deliverance 79
Crystal's Visitation 95
A Night of a Thousand Tears 107
The Lost Sheep 121
An Intervention for Miss Pris 135
Yet We Can't Not 151

Afterword 161

Up the Hill

If it makes things any easier, think of it as a welcome wagon. When newbies get lugged up here, our people show up, as they have for a decades, I'm told, even though I've only been here eighteen years in human time, which seems like no time at all, but then being dead-and-gone means you catch a substantial break when it comes to reading clocks.

I was saying you can think of it as a welcome wagon, but it's nothing more or less than a volunteer committee with rotating membership. Dying is a shock to most of us, in part because nobody knows time and place or what exactly comes after, really, even though there are as many scenarios as there are visions of them. Here's the thing: Sometimes the novices got to be nursed along because, first crack out of the box, they think they're alone and they aren't. We're a community, and those of us who've been around the block have learned some things that can keep the various annoyances at bay, you might say.

And we told him, Casey Aardappel, a square-shouldered old trucker – we let him know on our initial visit that it wasn't a good idea to keep your beloved on radar, nor to spend all your time pining after her, in the way that dead people can. It's understandable, even human (if I can use that word) to want stay behind, and it's not a Lot's wife kind of thing exactly, either (if you look back, *poof!* you're a pillar of salt); it's not that. It's just not smart.

We don't know everything, exactly. I mean, we aren't God. There are concrete advantages to being here – a good round of horseshoes being just one of them. But you got to get your bearings, so to speak, and one of the finest bits of advice we dispense – caringly, I might add – is that if you left a sweetheart behind, it's a good idea to let her be, especially if you're too young, by rights, to be here. Poor Casey Aardappel, big and tough as he was, found that advice hard to take, but he wasn't the first.

One night a bunch of us were sitting around talking, and we decided, after some discussion, that maybe two in ten have really wonderful marriages. It's something we can talk about now, even if the old man or old lady is right there beside us.

I couldn't help thinking how remarkable it was to see how free all of us marrieds are post-mortem. The old black-and-blue spots are gone, vanished, like they say. Here's the consensus we came to: one in ten marriages is pure disaster right from the get-go, three or four should probably never have hooked up, another three or four have some rich times along the line, and what's left are the few truly blessed. It's unscientific, but we like to think of ourselves as having a leg up on good old wisdom, something few of the folks down the hill know much of. Two marriages – maybe three – are really made in heaven, we decided. Which is not to say that if you had to do the whole thing over, several more than those couples truly blessed would still opt to get aboard the same train, all things being equal.

Me and Sarah, for one. These days we're more connected at the hip than we were for most of our marriage. I'm serious. And that's good, too.

The whole group of us finally decided that Casey, the new kid on the block, was one of those truly blessed. What's worse, he got himself sent here after a truck accident most of us chalked up to icy roads, even though he himself says he shouldn't have been on the highway that late, in that awful weather; and he wouldn't have been, if he hadn't wanted so badly to get home to Marcia, who was, of course, the solitary love of his life, emphasis on *was*. That's the very truth that's hard for some to grab hold of, understandably. I mean, the whole long-face thing was sad, as it always is; up here, we're not without feelings, after all.

As I was saying, me and my wife get along much better up here than we did down there, which isn't unusual, and would be something a goodly number of the folks we left behind could look forward to if they had the smarts, which they don't, sadly. When I first arrived, I used to hover around sometime just to bug her, like I always did – but that's a story for another time.

There Casey sat one night looking like a kid who'd just lost his dog, maybe two months after getting a place up here on the hill. He's a huge man, shoulders like the cab of that Peterbilt he loved.

"She looks in the mirror a whole lot more than she ever did that I remember," he told me when I stopped by a month or so after he showed up. "Every time I look, there she is again primping," he said.

"Don't watch," I told him for the eleventy-seventh time.

"Easier said than done," he told me. "Maybe she's crying; it happens."

"Not the way she turns her head, you know – brushes her hair, takes out a little stick of something and darkens her eyebrows. I don't think she ever gave a hang about her eyebrows. I know I didn't."

It was mid-summer, so he'd taken off that coat, and it was lying neatly over the stone. It hadn't taken long for us to notice that Casey Aardappel wasn't going to ruin the neighborhood. He kept his place up as well as any, despite the fact that he was here alone.

"We warned you about keeping a close eye," I told him. "I know it's tough for the first little while, but life up here'll be much easier if you stop at the river when you go down the hill – drop a line in or smoke that pipe of yours, but just don't go hanging around town and watching her all the time."

"Just about kills me," he said.

"I know," I told him. "We've all been there."

And then it came out.

"She bought a new bed," he told me.

I took a deep breath because the man was already costing us a ton of vigilance. "Look," I said, "the fact is, once they get insurance money, they're not always responsible for what happens, see? Some of 'em – your Marcia among 'em – probably never had that kind of bucks before."

"Still," he said.

"*Still* nothing," I told him. "You're gone now, at least to her mind."

"That hurts," he said.

"Sure it does," I told him, "but give her some wiggle room. We were saying just the other night what a fine couple the two of you made, right? You were there."

"A new bed?" he said.

"Didn't take long, and Marcia Van Gorp took a trip to Vegas with some old college friends," I told him because it was the truth. "We nearly had to stake old Gordy down." "Vegas?" he said.

I shrugged my shoulders. "She buy a Sealy or something really expensive?" I asked him. "What the heck is she planning, you think?"

"Stay out of her way, Casey," I told him.

But he couldn't, a sin for which he can be forgiven, if he can forgive himself.

Oh, yeah, and there was this too:

"Who the heck is Jenny Craig?" he asked me.

We're not all-knowing, if you're wondering, but we're blessed with some pretty cagey powers, given that time and space are largely irrelevant. The whole lot of us could blow this place in the twinkling of an eye, as the Bible says, and some do. More power to them. But some stay, like me and a host of others. I'm too connected to move. *Ach*, what am I saying? I could get to some Riviera beach faster than e-mail. Then what I am doing here? Good question. It's home, I guess.

Sue Ann Merced stayed, even though she was young enough to look pretty handy in a tank top. Disease, it was – cancer, something in a woman's variety, I guess. Left her husband, Mel, behind, the only rancher any of us ever knew not to have a farmer's tan, the kind of man who made other men cringe when he walked into a restaurant.

You guessed it: Sue Ann's Mel knocked on Marcia Aardappel's door after his people talked to her people, and, well, not all that long after Casey had got himself a place up here. Down there, of course, timing is a big deal – *how fast is too fast?*, and all of that. Timing doesn't mean much up here, of course, although I must admit that some of us did think that Mel might have waited another season or two.

My friend Lawrence, who's Yankton Sioux, says white people brood far too long. Look at the loons, he says, or the wolves; they scream and howl for a couple days, go half-crazy, and then it's pretty much over. He's probably right. All of which is to say, however, that some of us still did, in fact, raise an eyebrow when Marcia started looking at that Mel, the Marlboro Man rancher, with that same female look Casey saw her drawing up in their bathroom mirror. But we've seen worse.

What I'm saying is Mel's trying to date his wife was really tough on Casey. It's like shedding a winter coat, in a way – getting used to life up here, I mean. It just takes a while for the baggage of that mortal coil to wear away. Down there, of course, nobody thinks of us, not that we need sympathy. When things pop so fast the way they did with Mel and Marcia, when they go quick like that, nobody down there ever thinks of the better half who's sitting up here with a galloping case of emotional heartburn.

Now Sue Ann's been here a while longer, and furthermore, while that cancer went fast, she had lots of time to tell her husband before she died how to live once she'd departed. She says the whole business of another woman came up several times in those late-in-the-game, bedside conversations, and she told him he was the kind of man who couldn't really live all that joyfully, if alone. "Go find someone," she'd told him, but he hadn't – not 'til Casey died and his Marcia started tending her eyebrows all by her lonesome.

Sue Ann's not on the committee – the welcome-wagon thing – right now, but we're fluid up here, so we asked ourselves who could befriend poor Casey better than Sue Ann, right? That's what we were thinking. We appointed her to be something like an AA sponsor, to be there if needed – well, *when* needed. There comes a time when even the dead have to take life into our own hands.

So one night, the two of them decided to go to town together and play spectators, a very dangerous game. Sue Ann said she couldn't really keep him away, so she started to think that maybe if he just sat there and stared into the fire, he'd actually cool off a little. Sometimes you pull out all the stops.

And before we go any further, let me just say that to people who don't quite get it, all these extra powers we're blessed with are something of a mixed bag, at least at first. We get to see all kinds of stuff we never did. There ain't no closed doors. Life is the naked city, all right?

Which is why, once you're up here for a while, what we try to tell rookies is you really ought to stay put for a time. Talk about culture shock. From up here, what you once revered sometimes ends up looking more than a little silly. You get to understand why even the Lord God Almighty sometimes loses it at the goofiness of the whole human tribe.

Don't think of the two of them, Mel and Casey, as being in some divine hovercraft either. Remember *The Invisible Man*? Something like that, which is not to say that the two of them were actually *in* the restaurant at the same time as their spouses – I mean, no Ghostbusters would have spotted them. It's a mind thing, totally. You go there, in a way, even though you don't. It's complicated.

So on the night in question, it was Sue Ann playing nursemaid, you might say, to poor Casey, and I was on call. There are no phones, but it's all wireless, of course, so mobilizing is a snap, when necessary. And, okay, if I were Casey the trucker, I guess I would have been on edge myself because his Marcia (see what I just said? – "*his* Marcia"; she's no longer *his*, but habits die hard) – because *his* Marcia and Sue Ann's Mel went out for an Iowa chop at that new restaurant in Sibley, then left the parking lot and decided that as long as they were out, they'd take some county roads home and check the crops. Not unusual, of course; most widows and widowers get antsy about being seen by hometown folk, so they stay the heck out of Dodge.

Think of us – Casey anyway – as a kind of spiritual paparazzi.

Anyway, those first dates can hurt – I know that. We all do. We're not God-like, even though we do get more heavenly wisdom than you can imagine.

It was still early and plenty light out when Mel parked that Buick on the kind of road the county doesn't plow come December. It was one of those nights when a million stars roll out before you, and the moon rises like a Florida orange out East, too nice to hole up inside somewhere, especially since the two of them were sweetly furtive about what was going on between them. The whole thing could have been innocent enough, a kind of teaching moment for Casey, I'm thinking. And I was around, too – back-up, you might say – even though neither Sue Ann nor Casey the Possessed knew it right then. I'm not subject to untoward hovering – I mean, we are angels, so to speak – but this night had me antsy because poor Casey hadn't yet picked up the necessary defenses, and you don't want to risk some kind of silliness, which can happen, let me tell you.

Besides, what's a country walk under the stars anyway, right? Almost harmless. Some sweet nature study maybe, the corn and beans in perfect orderly rows beneath the bold moonlight, nothing out but wildlife. If there's anything I've learned since coming up here, it's that I sure as heck wished I'd taken more time for such things myself back then. Sarah, too.

But a man the size and power of Casey Aardappel can mix up something explosive, and we just don't want to operate in such a way as to bring people up here to our world, sweet as it is, before their due time.

I was on duty one night when Wendy Vermeer brought down a chandelier at a senior's dance when her husband – who used to get around even before she came up the hill – grabbed his partner's sweet behind in a fashion that made her (that is, Wendy) come alive, so to speak. I'm not joking – she brought down the chandelier. People could have been hurt.

Mostly we're limited by what's there. I mean, big Casey couldn't have just absconded with his precious Marcia, swiped her off that road as if it were the rapture; but even though the evening was windless, he could have raised a dust devil with little more than heavy breathing. Besides, the way I saw it, the only heavy breathing on that country road was coming from Casey himself.

I'm not blind to the fact that some deep moral lesson can be had in an evening's walk under the stars; and when people get as old as those two, they're normally susceptible to moral lessons and all manner of seriousness, unless their vision is beclouded. Big Casey must have seen the possibilities for seriousness in that solitary country walk. I mean, I know how he thinks. Been there, done that.

Anyway, it was a darling night out there in the country, deliciously warm, spacy clouds enough to catch colors from a sun already long gone. What I'm saying is I didn't mind hovering, beauty being so sumptuous up here, to us. But then, you wouldn't know about that.

And I'll grant you that a walk in the country air, beneath the stars, where the deer and the antelope play, is not just another day at the office. I mean, people who walk out there on a summer's eve got to like each other, and Casey knew it. We all did. So when Casey made a move toward those crows up the road, I grabbed his arm – I did it myself because what Sue Ann was working at wasn't exactly working out, and I just figured a little good cop, bad cop might be the trick.

"Let it go, Casey," I told him. I could feel the bull in his huge, tensed bicep. You might think death would empty out an ordinary supply of testosterone, but it's a funny world up here when you first arrive.

Honestly, Casey Aardappel couldn't even talk to me because he knew I knew – and so did Sue Ann – that he'd been thinking about stirring up a monsoon of crow excrement to dampen the enthusiasm over those two that night. He had to stare down his fears because the only way he'd get over his silliness was looking it right in the eye and smiling. We're not actual zombies, after all, even though the word may slip out now and then, only because it's fashionable. Like I said, we're angels, after a fashion.

Maybe I myself wish what happened next hadn't happened, but when the two of them – Casey's beloved and her new paramour – came back to the car, they stayed there, as in *parked*. I'm not kidding. That was something I hadn't expected, but when you hang around humans long enough, nothing surprises you after a while.

Now, nobody lives on that road, so I'm already trying to figure out what the devil Casey's going to go after now, maybe felling the cottonwood that spread its limbs over the Buick. Dangerous. And I know it's going to get worse because when Mel doesn't start the engine, but just stays there like some horny teenager, the match is an inch away from the Roman candle Casey has become, and there ain't no wind to douse it either.

Here's what experience has taught me. A man like Casey feels one of two emotions: Either he's suicidal and heartbroken, or he wants to break someone's skull, someone like Mel's. I knew what he'd fashioned with that flock of crows, so I wasn't thinking about hauling out Kleenex – yet.

With a man his size, I was scared to death, which is an expression that just doesn't work, I know.

Now all the while Sue Ann is there, and it's her husband in that Buick, too, remember, but she's a veteran herself, and I figure she's on my side.

Shoot Matilda, I was wrong.

Suddenly, we're all three of us in the back seat, there's steam coming out of Casey's ears, Sue Ann is biting her lip and getting weepy, and I'm sitting between them – behind the lovers – with my fingers on my cell phone (I don't have a cell, but you get the picture), ready to call in a flight of angels.

And here's the way the dialogue goes:

"I don't believe what I'm feeling," Marcia says up there in the front seat. "I wouldn't have believed it; if you'd told me a year ago or something that this could happen, I wouldn't have believed it. I honestly wouldn't have believed it."

I'm squashed between two basket cases. There's bucket seats up front, so Mel's arm is across the console and in her lap, where he's holding her hand. It's dark, and the dash lights are shining up across their faces. All Casey would have had to do is reach out arm's length, and he could have swatted a mosquito off the soft flesh of his beloved's bare neck.

I don't have to tell you that these lovers are aging. I mean, the tigers in their tanks have long since departed, which certainly doesn't mean that this night is over. It just means that we've got some time is what I'm saying, old folks' pacing being what it is.

"What she just said doesn't mean she loves you any less," I told Casey. "You heard her. She couldn't have guessed she could feel what she does a year ago – what she means is that she was deep in love with you."

Big Casey's not saying a word.

Now, Mel, who isn't dumb, isn't saying much either, because, like any male, he knows the action's got to arise in Marcia's heart first.

"She's not the first he's been with either," Sue Ann says to me, bitterly I might add, news I hadn't counted on. And I realize that this whole situation is just about out of control because Casey looks at her as if what she's just admitted about her own ex-husband is motive enough for the murder he's contemplating in his all-too-human heart *and* hands.

And just like that – *boom!* – my wife is in my lap, and now there's four of us where General Motors never meant any more than two.

"My word, Sarah," I said.

"So much like you," she says, "a guy who wouldn't read a map. You think you can pull this off all by your lonesome, don't you? My word, get these people out of here," she says, and just like that all four of us are at the side of the road. I know you know Casey's a big, big man, but there are things I just can't explain. It's something like levitation, but not totally.

"If you ask me," my wife says, "we're all better off heading back up the hill for a cup of coffee and a donut."

But Casey wasn't about to move. There he sat in the dirt, this huge trucker on his butt at the side of the road, legs splayed, and fingers full of ditch grass. Did I tell you he used to drive truck? – not just pick-ups either, eighteen-wheelers. Barrel-chested, a head of hair to die for, and there he sits like a sullen kid in a sandbox.

Think of it this way – we're in a split-screen world, so while the four of us were situated outside the warm environs of that Park Avenue, we're still within earshot. Just down the road, four or five deer come out of the corn and stare up the car that's catching the moon's glow. Somewhere off behind us, there's coyotes singing at each other, and I'm thinking that all we need right now is a skunk to stroll through.

"I think we got to start here," Mel the rancher said to Marcia. "We got to start with the fact that both of us lost big-time," he told her. "Both of us, and we can't replace what's gone."

Marcia looked up at him with cow eyes.

"I know my Sue Ann and I talked about it some," he told her. "I mean, in those last days, it came up because she brought it up – how she thought I'd need someone, being who I am."

"Did that hurt?" Marcia asked him. They were already holding hands.

My wife plopped herself down beside Casey, just sat there as if they were both in that sandbox.

"Of course," Mel told Marcia. "You know how it is in those times – you can't see beyond your nose, you know – all you think about is how you can't lose her that way, how you can't live without her."

It was dark in that car, really dark, and we can't see everything, either, but when Mel reached over to the glove compartment and pulled out one of those little cellophane packages of Kleenex, we all knew it was Marcia who was tearing up, still holding his hand, but tearing up. That had to be a good thing, I thought, at least it had Casey looking up instead of down.

"Sometimes I feel as if I'm doing something wrong, but how can it be wrong when it feels so right?" Marcia said, dotting at her nose and eyes.

I know for a fact that the woman hasn't listened to country-western music for four decades. What she said was coming out of someplace real.

"It's like there's two voices," Mel told her. "I hear 'em too."

And now my wife has hold of Casey's hand, and Sue Ann has mine, and this whole thing is turning into something bordering on *Dr. Phil*.

"What do you think Casey would say if he could see us right now?" Mel said.

"He'd want me happy," Marcia told him. "That much I know – my husband would want me happy."

"That's what I want," Sue Ann told me. She had my hand in both of hers, as if a wind might just blow her away. "That's what I told him, too, before I died," she said, pulling me toward her as if to be sure I was looking in her eyes to read the truth. "We talked about it – he and I did. And that's what I told him."

"I mean, right now – the two of us, out here on this road in the middle of nowhere," Mel said. " – what d'you think Casey would say? You think he'd say, 'go for it, sweetheart'?" "He never once called me 'sweetheart,'" she told him.

"Never?"

Sarah kept hold of Casey because maybe he didn't need to hear that.

"He had his ways of showing he loved me," Marcia told him. "He had his ways."

"So did my wife," Mel told her, and with that Sue Ann let go of my hand and walked over to Sarah and Casey – he was *her* assignment, remember?

"It's strange, isn't it? – but I still can't help think that she's around," Mel said. "I come out of the family room and into the kitchen, and I'm actually surprised that she's not there, like always. I wake up at night and reach for her, as if she'd never left – almost by instinct."

So I go over and get down on my haunches, like I couldn't do for most of my life, I might add, and I'm sitting there along with everyone else, all of us around Casey, as if it we're about to do some serious laying-on-of-hands, which is, after a fashion, what we're doing, all three of us. But it's not us that's bringing him back to life and reason – it's what he's hearing. So Casey gets to his feet, and just like that, all four of us wedge our way into the back seat once again, as if every little word is too valuable to miss.

"Me?" Marcia says, " – I spent too much of my life alone, anyway, with him always on the road. It's not like that," she says to Mel, "because I'm so accustomed to being alone since the kids left and Casey normally gone for a week or so at a stretch."

And I know for a fact that Casey was one of those men truly blessed to love what he did with his life: the man loved the road, loved hauling cattle, loved watching the sun come up some place in Utah or over the Great Smokies or wherever.

"You didn't like it?" Mel asked, "him being gone like that?"

"It's what he loved," she told him. "If I wouldn't have let him be, I wouldn't have loved him as much as I did."

"You hear that?" I said to Casey. "You hear what she just said?"

And for that my wife pinched me, which is, just like it's always been, her way of saying shut up.

"Still," Marcia told him, "almost every night I look up at the clock to see how long it'll be until nine or so, when he used to make it home. It's a habit with me, and I got to tell myself," she stopped to reach for another Kleenex, " – I have to remind myself that he's not coming back, that he's not out somewhere west of the river in South Dakota, or wherever, that he's not going to call any minute like he always did to let me know he's going to be late." There was so much pain in that woman's voice that I thought right then, our man Casey had to be well down the road toward a cure. "And there's no flowers on the coffee table, either," she told him.

"Flowers?" Mel said.

"A rule he had – if he'd be gone three days, he'd send flowers – three days, flowers – three days, flowers. All the time."

I swear at that moment, both my wife and Sue Ann would have married Casey Aardappel in a minute, the two of them all over him like some up-north down comforter, my wife Sarah lifting an eyebrow at me in a manner I understood altogether too well. And I'm thinking, "Who knew that barrel-chested trucker, big enough to body slam a sow, was sending roses to his sweetheart for all those years of marriage? Who would have guessed?" He was – they were – one of the few so truly blessed.

Now Casey wasn't saying a thing, but his body temperature – well, he's got none really, but you know what I mean – was such that I swear I could tell things were cooling inside.

"I miss him every hour of every day," Marcia told Mel, and then she went on from there into something that made the dirt on that road into pure gold: "Sometimes I look in the bathroom mirror," she said, "thinking of him coming home, you know, late at night, like he used to. I put on some eye-liner, touch up the lipstick, and for a moment, like always, I just think he's coming near – or he's already there, right behind me. Sometime I swear he is. I miss him more than anything."

Then there was silence. Mel put his arm up around her, and I thought it was a gallant thing to do.

Listen, you get talents post-mortem that you won't believe, but we can't tell people down the hill what to say, although sometimes, as you can well imagine, we'd love to.

And right then, Casey said the only thing he did all night long, as I remember. "Maybe it's time now for me to go," he said, nodding his head, as if the battle was won.

And just like that the four of us were back outside the car in the glow of a silver moon and a black sky inlaid with a million diamonds. "Come on," my Sarah said. "Lets us go back up the hill – it's a gorgeous night."

Three times, maybe, that huge guy wiped that big hand of his through that shock of silver hair that glowed, as if on purpose, out there in the country, and he never once looked at any of us, not me or the ladies, just stared out into the darkness and the long angling rows of corn and soybeans running out before us in the midsummer's moonlit darkness like the grain of an old oak table. I don't really remember more than a line or two Casey said all night long as we sat there gawking and listening in to a dialogue the Lord God almighty played for him, so close to perfection it was.

"Let's go home," Sue Ann said, smiling. I almost forgot that it wasn't the easiest night for her, either, even though she's been gone a whole lot longer than Casey. She'd heard more than she'd come to hear.

So three of us started up that abandoned road together, thinking Casey wasn't about to stay put behind us, assuming that he was, as he'd already admitted, ready to go now, as we were. His sweet Marcia didn't love him one bit less for his being gone.

I thought it was over. I really did.

But he didn't leave: For two minutes, maybe more, he just stood there, looking up at the moon, staring into space, almost as if he was praying, which he might have been doing, something that comes a whole lot easier to us these days, by the way. And then he walked off into the corn. Just walked away.

My wife took hold of Sue Ann's arm as if to tell her to let him be, not to go after him now because we'd only be enabling him if we'd once again started chasing him. Even a dead man has to have a moment or two in his own holy of holies, I thought. Besides, what's he going to hurt out there in the corn?

He walked out into that field, that Peterbilt of a man, and disappeared into tassels way higher than his head; and we let him be a few minutes, until what came out of that eighty acres was a howl so long and broad and arching that no man in his right mind could have guessed it was only a coyote, though that was the voice of the creature he chose. Honestly, I've never heard anything so unearthly, and that's saying something for a dead man. I have no idea what Mel and Marcia thought inside that Buick, but it wasn't more than a flash until down the road they went, away from us, in a cloud of dust.

And then, just like that, Casey walked out again, came out of that field like Shoeless Joe, walked out like a dead man alive to a new life, a smile on his broad Dutch face, as if to say that this isn't Iowa at all, but Heaven.

That's what I saw happen. All night long, I honestly don't know that he'd said much more than a word – just howled. And it wouldn't be the first time I've thought long and hard about how we missed something in not picking up some wisdom from the Yankton Sioux, who lived out here hundreds of years before we ever came along.

We could've been back up the hill in a flash, of course, but we chose to walk that night, the sky being so full of stars, the moon already climbing high enough to cast lovely shadows across the dirt road in front of us from the tall corn on the south side.

By the time we got back up the hill, I had a healthy handful of prairie coneflowers, along with some wild bergamot, and a garland of phlox for my wife because today, even though I live where I do, I want to tell you that I certainly am a whole lot smarter than I once was. I still know how to be married. Flowers were in order, I thought.

But then, up here, they always are.

The Unveiled

It should come as no surprise that death creates some unlikely bedfellows. Up here, up the hill, sworn enemies share a morning pot of coffee. The three Vande Gaard brothers, who fell into ten years of silence after their father's will was read, hang out here along the river as if they were boys, just a mile downstream from the home place.

A cemetery is as democratic as a public school: we've got to take everybody. One of the blessings of being dead and gone is miserable long-standing grudges melt away like a late April blizzard.

I bring it up because everyone here knows the story of little Scotty deVries, who, just a year ago, took his own life one night when his mother was, oddly enough, attending a PTA meeting and his father was who-knows-where. Scotty, just 13 years old, hung himself in his bedroom. Emotionally, he'd been picked to pieces by tough-guy bullies, not unlike a score of other kids who were somehow blessed with the wherewithal to suffer through their own tortures. Overweight and friendless, as un-athletic as some hunched octogenarian, Scotty deVries threw in the towel, and for maybe six weeks or so, waves of tearful introspection rolled like floodwaters into and over the town – nowhere near long enough, or so our sages calculated.

If I'd been down there still, running the newspaper, Scotty's obit would have been something I'd have had to cut back on, even falsify. And that's another reason to love my new digs – ours. Up here, the truth can not only be told, but accepted, because we are, you remember, far more forgiving than the living, which doesn't mean we weren't as torn up about Scotty taking his own life as anyone down the hill, although probably less so, life itself not being quite so precious here – it being, so to speak, behind us. I know to say it's been good for the boy to be with us sounds unfeeling, but up here on this more forgiving side of the divide he's, well, blossomed.

And strangely enough by your standards – I'm sorry for straying so far from the point – he now has an unlikely best buddy, his own great-grandma, a woman he'd never known, a woman who'd seen his travail, including the moment he'd taken that step off his desk chair. She was, in fact, the first to speak to him, to let him know he wasn't alone up here.

What's more, that great-grandma of his is my mother.

"Scotty," she told him that day, "it's just so nice to meet you." He was sitting in the grass, looking down the hill toward town, sitting there like the child he had been. "I'm your grandma's mother," my mother told him, " – your Grandma Van Kempema's mom."

Sometimes it helps to be young. When old farts come up here, they have some trouble tuning into the fact that, in some ways, they're still around. Scotty smiled as if what she'd announced wasn't really much of a surprise at all.

"We lived six miles west," she pointed up the road, "and a half south, a place with a big grove, even then, eighty years ago," she told him.

Scotty, startlingly, seemed at home with the idea that up here he was talking to a woman a century older than he was, yet someone who loved him. "I've seen your picture," he told his great-grandma. "You were wearing a hat, for Sunday. You were going to church."

"I don't think Mother would have allowed us to use a camera on the Sabbath," she told him. "Might have been a funeral or a wedding."

He pulled both legs up beneath him. "There was a wagon behind you – horses." "Next time I'll have to look," she told him, as if it were a promise.

"You been to my house?" he asked.

"You're my family," she told him, and then she got down on the grass beside him. "You feeling better?" she asked him.

His blue eyes got dreamy. "You know about what happened?" he asked. "We all know," she told him.

He looked up behind her. "There's more of you?" "Look around," she told him.

He saw no one but the hundreds of stones he couldn't have missed. He scratched his head.

"It's not something I thought of then," he told her, pointing toward town, "but up here, I'm thinking about what I did – and I still think it was the right thing, you know –"

My mother nodded grudgingly.

"What I did – I hope it changes things," he told her. "I wasn't thinking of that – that's not it," he told her, sadly. "I'm saying *now*, sitting up here like this, whoever I am right now – what I'm saying is that I hope it does them all some good." Mostly I think he was confused, as all of us are first thing. "You're dead too, aren't you?" he said to his great-grandma. "You understand?" "Things look different, sure," my mother told him.

"That's not why I did it," he told her, and she reached for him then, put her hand on his. "I wasn't thinking how I wanted to get back at them or that maybe it would be good for them – that's not it."

"I know," she told him.

"It was that, to me, mornings all seemed dark as night," he told her. His eyes scanned her whole face, top to bottom. "You sure you're my grandma?"

"You got my blood in you – or did," she told him. She opened her hand to him as if it were right there in her life lines.

"This isn't hell, is it?" he asked.

My mother put her arm around him, her hand on the back of his neck, and pulled him, like a mother, into her chest. She'd asked me to be there just in case she might need backup, so to speak, and I hope it comes as no surprise to you when I say that my mother, who died already a half-century ago and never knew this boy at all, nor his parents, sat there in the grass shedding tears, and tried her best to wipe them away the moment they appeared. "No, dear," she told him, "this for sure isn't hell."

Scotty came to us alone, even though no one is, and my mother made sure he wasn't. We all watched that day and found it sweet; but then, up here we're not all that hard to please.

It was my mother's idea to go to church that Sunday evening, when Scotty's father, who'd been a loose live-r, to say the least, had determined that the faith he'd been born into and walked away from was now calling him back, once again, after Scotty took his own life. He wanted to testify in the very church he'd spurned for lo, these many years. My mother determined that Scotty should go with.

We've got church up here, too, but some distinctions are simply lost post-mortem. No one here defines *worship* as something that happens only between four walls, nor in the presence of a pulpit or Communion table. Besides, we're all preachers, though, truth be known, we've still got our favorites. What I'm saying is no one here feels compelled to go down the hill to enter a sanctuary, not like in real life, which is not to say this isn't. Try to imagine a world in which the practice of piety is always real. It's quite heavenly.

If I had it to do all over again – and this isn't wishful thinking because, believe me, we're not subject to that kind of envy – I would have tried harder to be a real writer, taken the idea of writing stories more seriously when I was down the hill because I never realized, until I made it up here, how richly all those human lives played out before me, even then, whole novels through the generations. I understand it now – just as I understand so much. If I was still down there, with what I know I could write a whole lot better novel than the one attempt I made, because some lines from the Old Testament make more sense these days – the sins of the father and all of that, the legacy we leave behind. Nobody up here blamed Scotty's father for what his son did – nobody. The good Lord be thanked, we're beyond blaming. But down there, what wasn't said aloud could have created an ice jam in late July.

My mother insisted on sneaking down the hill and attending worship that night because her granddaughter's husband – Scotty's father – wanted to testify to the faith he'd found again after the horror of his son's taking his own life. And she wanted Scotty to be there, too. And her husband. And me. And whoever else was around and interested. That night we could have used a school bus because that church turned into a massive congregation of saints.

Around here, the second Sabbath worship, an evening service, isn't well-attended anymore, so for those few from town who showed up, the old church, as usual, seemed achingly bereft. But there were tons of us because everyone had seen how lovingly she'd taken her great-grandson in, not that it was a burden – burdens having been lifted, remember. Besides, most of us had nothing else scheduled.

Scotty's father, my sister's son-in-law, makes money and loses it, almost as a way of life.

He's never seen a fad he wouldn't buy into – blown-in insulation, heat pellets made from waste, even ethanol. He's first on board, and he's built more big houses, and lost them, than most people find time to covet. He's either rich or bankrupt, an insanely purposeless talker who has more enemies than you can shake a stick at.

He takes people with him – good times and bad – and when others are timid, Turkey deVries, he's nicknamed, doesn't hesitate. He's hungry as a jackal, got eyes like a raptor, and the sweet words of a crooked preacher. He stays in Highland only because it's home, the place where we've got to take him back. And we have.

Turkey never knew what to do with little Scotty, who wasn't cut out of the same sharp steel that he is. He's the kind of man who will never win public office, even though he's always running. Let's just be clear about things here – what people have always said about Turkey deVries I couldn't have put in my paper. He's an asshole, all right. I couldn't have printed that, and I probably shouldn't say it now, given my status; but I can because there are things you know once you're dead. Trust me.

It was the end of winter, that time of year when everybody's sick of cold because the warm promise of southern breezes is growing ever more immediate. It was January cold, even though it was almost March, a fierce wind out of the northwest, following two or three days of spotty snowfall, fleece-like, and weightless.

When there were more people on the land out here – more farms, more houses, more big families – the church was a whole lot bigger, the balcony – Sunday morning or Sunday night – nearly always full. Today, that spacious upstairs section is rarely used, so that's where we all went that night, up in the balcony – a half-dozen rows of curious, saintly zombies, some of us arriving earlier than others, just like the old days because old habits die hard. Gerrit Bosma was first. He waited outside just like he always did in real life, his family in the Buick.

Among the living, no one really believed Turkey's latest profession of faith because most people stopped believing anything from his mouth a couple decades ago. So even though that old church hasn't been full for forty years or more at evening worship, the crowd that night made the nave look like eighty acres of corn *after* harvest, here and there a half-dozen yellowing stalks over shorn rows so straight you could have shaved with them. Most people stayed home to avoid acid reflux.

Here comes the hard part. You've got to grant us some omniscience, hard as that might be for you to understand. We don't know everything, but we know more than we ever did, and that's a blessing. None of us hang out at casinos across the river anymore – those poor Lakota would have to lock the doors. But there is no greed up here. I'm not asking you to believe me, but we've got crystal balls that work a whole lot better than the ones we used to think we had down the road.

Here's the thing: we know the truth. Mother insisted on going down the hill and getting a place for her and Scotty, front row, in that empty balcony because she did. She knew, all of us did, that this time – impossible as it was to believe for anyone down there, including Turkey's wife, my sister's daughter – what Scotty had done had grabbed that man's heart in its iron fist and squeezed until nothing bled from it, nothing at all. It wasn't the first time Turkey de Vries had gone down on his knees, believe me, but this time he'd done it because he couldn't stand for one more minute on his own two feet of clay. What Scotty did scrubbed that damned pride away with an acid wash.

So we knew that this time his penitence was for real, even though nobody else in that sanctuary did. No one. Not the preacher, Pastor De Graaf, a kind old man people up here trust because he visits, often. Not Turkey's daughter, Scotty's sister. Not his neighbors. Not even Pammy, his wife. Nobody knew that this time the sinner standing up before that measly crowd wasn't lying – to others or to himself.

Trust me. We see things you don't.

I'm wanting to tell this story right, and I don't know if it's coming along the way it should, either, not ever having written things like this because in a lifetime as a small-town journalist, too often I couldn't tell the whole truth and nothing but – and this one, Turkey's readmission to the sacraments – wouldn't have made the *Weekly* anyway, even though it might have been a good headline. It's just another amazing thing that happened that I can't get out of my mind. Praise God.

Rev. De Graaf had to dig that odd readmission form out of a dust-laden hymnal, because thumbing people out the church stopped about the time church horse barns got auctioned away and hauled off with mules. It doesn't happen anymore that men or women are actually excommunicated; when they get in trouble, they just pick up their papers and do church business elsewhere, some place they're thankfully forgotten. I admit it: it was like Turkey to want this whole deal public.

Look, it's hard not to dislike him – I'll admit that – but like I say, we knew that this time he was telling the whole truth, so help me God, because what he saw inside himself after his son's death was a deepened shade of darkness he'd never seen before.

Every time Rev. De Graaf comes up the hill, he draws a silent crowd. He never sheds a tear, but he can stand before a grave like a night watchman, as if waiting, maybe, for a trumpet. I think he's one of the few around who seems to know, when he's here, that we are.

The old form from that dusty hymnal was something he could doctor up a bit to make it relevant to Turkey's story, which he did. Lenora Ooms was at the organ that night, an old family friend of my sister's. Five rows of empty pews stood between the pastor and a half dozen silver-haired men and women, who weren't there for the ceremony, but wouldn't miss worship even if that night they were forced to witness something almost distasteful. Credit the old preacher, who'd scheduled the ceremony for the evening service, not the morning when, without a doubt, Turkey would have been an awful distraction.

There were three families with little kids, nary a high-schooler – they're all in the with-it church on the other side of town – a half dozen singles, and, of course, Pammy, Turkey's longsuffering wife. And three or four of her coffee friends, not members, showed up for moral support.

And us, a balcony full of ghosts.

The old pastor slipped on his reading glasses.

"Beloved Christians," he said. We'd sung a few hymns, prayed, and taken an offering. The sermon was to come. "We have lately informed you of the conversion of our fellow-member Gerrit de Vries, to the end that with your approbation he might be received again into the Church of Christ."

And so it began, Turkey standing up all alone, his wife Pammy sitting beside him. Some of us thought it might have been nice to see her stand there with her husband, but we knew that Pammy, like everyone else, wasn't all that confident of her husband's newfound righteousness. He had a long record, after all. Really, it's a wonder she was there, a wonder she wasn't already with us in the balcony. Mother would have liked that.

Ten months had passed, I think, their time.

"The Lord Christ, declares that whatsoever His ministers shall loose on earth shall be loosed in Heaven," the preacher said, gently, every last word savored. Hard to believe that, once upon a time, I thought him a bigot, but then it took death, in my case, to see that we all can change, some of us deeply blessed to get a head start before making it up here.

"Therefore, since God declares in His Word that He takes no pleasure in the death of the wicked, but rather that he should return from his way and live, the Church always hopes for the conversion of the backslidden sinner and keeps her bosom open to receive the penitent."

It seemed to me that the church keeping "her bosom open" couldn't be sung with the beat that comes from the drum set beside the piano, but De Graaf didn't run away from that language, either. He read it with a kind of solemn respect, as if God himself might have been speaking.

"But to proceed now to the matter in hand," he said, both hands beneath the hymnal. "I ask you, Gerrit deVries, do you declare with all your heart, here before God and His church, that you are sincerely sorry for your sin and stubbornness?" He waited for a couple of seconds, then did something unusual – stepped out from behind the pulpit and took a step down on the platform, as if to say there needed to be nothing between him and Turkey.

It was deathly quiet in that church – and I'm not making a pun. My mother was standing there holding her great-grandson, perfectly riveted on what was going on downstairs.

"Do you also truly believe that the Lord has forgiven you and does forgive your sins for Christ's sake?" the preacher said.

A half century or more may have passed since there was that much drama in that old church, and the silence alone created tears in the eyes of some people, even though most of them were wrung from the most tragic thing to happen in Highland in years, that thing being Scotty's suicide. Trust me, no one was crying for Turkey de Vries. It would be lovely to think that people were taken by God's grace offered freely, once again, to a man some folks thought didn't deserve a dime's worth. But that wasn't it. It was Scotty who, in a way – even for them – was there that night because he simply could not have been absent.

"And do you therefore desire to be readmitted to the Church of Christ," the pastor asked, "promising henceforth in all godliness, according to the command of the Lord?"

Three questions. Turkey stood there like Gibraltar, which is the way he wanted it.

Rev. De Graaf took another step down, and for a moment I wondered whether he'd walk right into the messiness and lay his hands on the man.

"I do," Turkey said, and nodded.

Not a soul in that church saw what Scotty did, felt what he felt, knew what he knew; and what I saw in the boy's eyes just then was nothing less than glory – trust me. But then, that boy is no longer a boy.

"We then, being here assembled in the Name and the authority of the Lord Christ, declare you, Gerrit de Vries, to stand in the communion of Christ," Rev. De Graaf said, one arm now raised, "of the holy sacraments, and of all the spiritual blessings and benefits of God which he promises to and bestows upon His Church."

And then he did it, that Pastor I once disliked – he walked right down the aisle to where Turkey was standing, shook his hand, grabbed his shoulder, and pulled him into a hug.

And then Pammy, too, because that old pastor wanted to show that sparse crowd that he was buying the whole thing and ready to invest in this man who'd been broken like few can be. I'm sure the next day, that the coffee shop, sixty-five other conversations, were full of talk about how Pastor John de Graaf at that moment grabbed Pammy's hand and put it in her husband's, pulling them together, as if they were getting hitched all over again.

It was heavenly really, even though people said the next day – not up here, but down there – that what they'd seen that night in the old church wasn't like anything that had happened in that church for a century at least, if ever – as if they knew.

But then Pammy quietly took her hand from her husband's and sat back down, a cue – it seemed to all of us – that everyone else needed to do the same, to end it, as if that much emotion let loose in the old church could prove dangerous to Turkey. She was scared. She's my own sister's child and, Lord knows, she's seen enough. She needed it to stop for a dozen reasons at least.

It was the very first moment since I've been up the hill that I told myself that someone I know down there really needed to be up here. If I could have taken Pammy up into the balcony just then, I swear I would have – but we have our rules. If the whole lot of us could have swept down there like an army, we would have. Nobody I know ever needed peace like she did right then. That's why she made it stop, and we knew it.

The old pastor backed off, nodding, as if to say he really shouldn't have tried to choreograph what happened, that he was pushing it himself, even though we all knew, upstairs, that he knew, as we did, that the man who'd just sworn his allegiance to God and his kingdom wasn't trying one more time, snake-like, to gather disciples.

Rev. De Graaf took one step up on the platform and opened the hymnal. "Gracious God and Father, we thank Thee through Jesus Christ that Thou hast given this, our fellow-brother, repentance unto life, and causest us to rejoice in his conversion." All those "thees" and "thous," he hadn't bother to edit. "We beseech Thee, show him Thy grace, that he may become more and more assured in his mind of the remission of his sins, and may derive therefrom joy unspeakable and delight to serve Thee."

Then the Lord's Prayer, in which we joined in, silently – I mean the balcony choir.

De Graaf took a drink from his glass and, with a thumbnail, wiped away a tear. I saw it. We all did. He had his Bible open to a passage in Second Corinthians, something he'd chosen earlier. "...Whenever anyone turns to the Lord," he read, "the veil is taken away."

My mother, in her silly church hat, and her grandson, Scotty, were the only ones standing now, just the two of them and, down below, good old Rev. De Graaf.

"And we, who with unveiled faces all reflect the Lord's glory, are being transformed into his likeness with ever-increasing glory, which comes from the Lord," he read, "who is the Spirit."

I swear he knew we were there. He was talking to the people out front, but what he read fell on our ears just as surely, maybe more so.

"Let's sing," he said, picking up the hymnal. "'Beautiful Savior,'" he said, "number 373," and Mrs. Ooms started on an intro.

What I don't know is how De Graaf knew – or if, in fact, he did. Maybe his choice was entirely his own. Maybe he'd asked Turkey for a favorite, maybe Pammy. I just don't know. What I know is that in an old hymnal I grabbed from my mother's shelf when she died, an old hymnal that I kept for years afterwards, a book that probably sits in my sister's house if she kept it, if she didn't simply toss it out, and if it's not burned in some incinerator or aging fretfully somewhere in the bowels of that landfill south of Sheldon – in that old hymnal, I remember a list of favorite hymns – Dad's, Mom's, Annie's, Gert's, and Jack's – all of them penciled into the inside cover in Mom's royally perfect hand, and Mom's, all of this dated, 1940, is "Beautiful Savior."

The preacher raised his hands during that song in a fashion that's almost never is done around here, and his eyes followed his left arm all the way to his fingertips, as if he really had no control, as if his hands had just found their way up there all by themselves, some other force lifting them and him, and this is what I saw: he looked directly at my mother and Scotty, the boy she was holding, and then back down at Pammy, his mother.

I don't know that my mother ever saw it, because she was thinking about Pammy, Turkey's longsuffering wife, Scotty's mom.

And then came the miracle: Pammy herself right then looked up at the balcony.

Maybe she was following the pastor's eyes – I don't know. But there was no one up here but us saints, the dead, but not gone, the ghostly audience who'd come down from the hill, as righteously as anyone, to witness the lost sheep returned, by grace, to the fold.

But Pammy wasn't seeing me or them or anyone suited up in angel wings or halos. What she saw – I swear it – was an ancient grandma she knew only by an old picture that hangs there in the family room, that very old grandma with her loving arm around her very own boy.

For the life of me, or the death of me, I'm still not sure how, or what, old De Graaf pulled off that night with God Almighty, and maybe my mother, too. I don't know what kind of bargain he struck, but somehow, some way, some incandescent light from a source I know as divine opened up on her grandma in that old church hat and her own boy standing straighter than he ever had in life itself. There they were, from a cloud, witnesses for Pammy de Vries.

No one in that church saw it like we did. It was a stunt old De Graaf somehow pulled off just for her, a woman who needed a blessed vision more than any other hungry soul that night.

When De Graaf's eyes swung quickly up toward the balcony once more, I gave him a thumbs up.

Last Tuesday he was back here up the hill. For a while, he stood at Scotty's grave, wearing a wizened smile I thought was just about as ripe with grace as even I could have ever imagined. There he stood. We all saw him. Like I said, he draws a crowd.

I still don't know what happened that night, but it doesn't bug me because up here, wonders never cease. They're just part of life, which is to say, I guess, they're just part of death. And all I know is, it's a joy.

I think I got that all right.

The Music of the Spheres

This is what we know: Mins de Boom spent thirty-seven years of his life in school, but never received a formal education. No one, not even his mother, ever thought of him as particularly keen. For thirty years, he worked in town as the school janitor. He spent only seven years as a student himself, and those years passed long ago when he was a boy in the country of his birth, the Netherlands, before the war, and before he immigrated.

We love Mins. We love universally, of course, hard as that may be to believe, but that doesn't mean we don't have favorites, and, trust me, Mins is right up there.

In the small Dutch town where Mins grew up, his mother died in her rocking chair on a Saturday afternoon in 1947 while smiling and seemingly contented, having just concluded her housecleaning, something she did always with religious devotion. Her house in order, she'd sat down, prepared as she was at that very moment of every week for death or the Sabbath, whichever came first.

That was two years after the war and four years after Mins's father had been deported to Germany by Nazis, never to return. With his mother gone and the country in shambles, what was left for Mins but emigration? So much he told us long ago, when we were still around, down the hill.

Long before the war, distant family had immigrated to a place called "Iowa," he said, and often, he'd tried to draw his lips into the position it took to pronounce such a strange word. Was a joy to see, really.

When he arrived in New York, he called his Uncle John in Iowa. "John," he said, "I'm here. Come get me." He didn't understand America to be such a huge place.

His Uncle John found Mins that job as a janitor in the school, where he would arrive each day before the students, look over the list of tasks he'd written up for himself the day before, and start in on washrooms, doormats, and windows that were forever smudged from children's dirty hands. Once classes began, he loved the silence in the empty corridors, the attentive humming behind every closed door, children busy learning, the world he knew in harmony. At the end of the day, with the blackboards clean and hallways shining, Mins assessed his little corner of God's creation and pronounced it very good.

The truth is, Mins de Boom was almost a bit too simple to be a sinner, the kind of man, therefore, the world has little use for.

He had but one vice to speak of, an old-world custom: he smoked cigarettes – fat, lumpy things he rolled himself, a habit the school board tried to discourage him from practicing in school. But on cold days, years ago, when he couldn't sneak out back of the school's machine shop, he would sit in the boiler room once classes had begun and have his first smoke. From a heavenly perspective, it wasn't much of a vice, really. We've seen much worse.

Sometimes the high school boys kidded him. "Hey, Mins," they'd say, "how about you roll us a joint?" Mins would squint and smile and shrug his shoulders. "I only been here yet thirty years," he'd say. "I don't know the language so good."

He came from a place in Holland where the Dutch themselves consider folks to be narrow and backward; and after his only relative in the States, Uncle John, had passed on, he had no opportunity to grow. He despised television and loved the church. Perhaps *love* isn't the right word. Worship, to Mins, was something as essential as breath, as making sure he lived an orderly life. After all, what he knew in his childhood was war.

The truth is Mins was much loved as a janitor, and when he retired the school board gave him a gold watch he wore only on Sunday. He treasured that watch more than anything he had ever been given in life – other than his wife, that is, whose feelings hadn't always been reciprocal.

All of that we didn't have to die to discover, chapters of the quiet legend Mins became, known to only a few, largely because most didn't care.

It may surprise you to hear that such a simple man as Mins would find a wife, but he married Lena Mars because he thought her children needed a father – and, after all, he was alone and therefore also eligible. She consented, or so people say, for something of the same reason and, after all, with her ex-husband's dismal record of child support, living with Mins was preferable, in Highland especially, to the public dole.

Her former husband had left with another woman, and while everyone in the church where both of them worshipped felt that what the man had done was an abomination, most of them secretly felt her husband's actions understandable, given Lena's shrill tongue and deep moodiness – gifts, as people said, she came by honestly, after all, if you knew her parents.

In a very good sense, their marriage was a matter of convenience, a case of two single people deciding to put away their loneliness.

And the truth is, no one knew much about the marriage of Mins and Lena, and although no one can really know for sure what happens in any bedroom save his or her own, such a fact didn't keep us from speculating, when we were still alive. Most the town guessed, back then, the marriage was consummated several times that first year, maybe occasionally the next, and almost certainly never thereafter, when, nightly, the neighbors began to see lights in two bedrooms turned out almost simultaneously.

People may think what they will, of course. And let me just add that about such things these days, we no longer speculate; and while that may sound awful, you need to remember that we're angels up here or we wouldn't be. Or something to that effect. We're not Peeping Toms, at least as you might understand such things.

Now Mins de Boom is no ordinary man. He did not marry Lena Mars out of all-consuming passion, nor even from some desire to heal his loneliness, a stranger, as he was, in a strange land. Psychologists might claim Mins himself had no perception of his own motivations, that what he really wanted was less charitable at bottom, let us say, than libidinal. But those psychologists would need also to consider Lena carefully, a woman most men would say lit no libidinal fires.

Mins de Boom made an unusual American because he expected so little from life. Perhaps it was his old country ethos, or his lack of education; perhaps it was the war, when he'd spent weeks looking for food out in the country surrounding the little Dutch village, all through the Hunger Winter. Perhaps it was the time he'd spent hidden away in the storage space he built himself to hide from German roundups, the *razzias* that had already taken his father. Then again, perhaps it was his faith, which taught him that storing up treasures in huge Siouxland barns would only get him unceremoniously stuck in the eye of a needle.

When he married Lena, Mins never demanded the kind of intimacy thought normal by the standards of American television, standards he knew nothing of. Of course, he was already forty-five years old – she was ten years younger – and he harbored no dreams of procreation.

What's more, in the home in which he'd grown up, displays of affection were thought gypsy-ish, the mark of someone frivolous or unsteady.

And after the Germans took his father away forever, he'd missed seeing his mother's husband around at all; he had no patterns for marital love, save pure and dogged loyalty.

But then, this we knew, too – he was a man happy with very little of what the world thinks necessary. And he and Lena, after the initial tribulation of any newlyweds their age – maybe a bit more – began to appreciate each other, although quietly, for their mutual sturdiness, you might say.

When he retired last year, he didn't simply excuse himself from living, as some do. He decided to walk the country ditches and clean the highways of trash, scavenging for bottles and cans thrown there, in part, by students whose refuse he'd been retrieving for years already. After all those countless semesters inside, he wanted to be in the beautiful sunshine. Besides, each container was worth a nickel, and he was indefatigably frugal, but never sinfully so. But then, you'll have to remember that I'm hardly an objective narrator.

We still watch his goings out and his comings back, so to speak. He has an old bicycle, the kind popular twenty years ago – thick tires beneath a seat as wide as a Farmall's, and a wire-mesh basket leaning over the front handlebars, a sturdy style of bike quite popular in the Netherlands. Over the back fender he's affixed an additional pair of baskets, and he sewed for himself a very wide and deep nylon duffel bag he throws over his shoulders like a knapsack. Lena bought him a hat at a garage sale, a straw hat, a Panama, with a single white band, which he wears to keep the sun off his bald head. On hot days, he often wears one of several old mesh football jerseys he'd redeemed from the school trash, but never short pants. What would people say, anyway, in Holland, about a man who ran around with such crooked legs all bare?

He often comes up the road, pedaling way too hard for an old man, we often tell each other. If Mins doesn't start taking it easy up the hill, Garrett Verstrate said not long ago, he'll never leave. We all laughed. We can, you know. Sometimes I think maybe too often.

Mins de Boom keeps a weekly route – Monday, west to the Inwood blacktop; Tuesday, as far as he can go toward Highway 9; Wednesday, a couple of miles east, beyond 75; and Thursday, south, as far as he can go on the oil to Rock Valley. On Fridays, he hits the gravel around town, and on Saturday, he stays home with Lena to clean house. Sundays, of course, he goes to church.

He is not hard to spot, a sun-tanned scavenger, cleaning the roadside of refuse people throw unthinkingly from cars and trucks. What he finds in the ditches around town makes him only more certain that one of the doctrines of the faith with which he was reared is accurate to the human condition: original sin.

But now, our story. Let me just be sure to say that all of you are interesting, lest you think differently. I know this sounds discriminatory, but – even with our halos – some of you are just a bit more interesting than others. Time, you remember, we have a lot of. From up here, the shows are extraordinary. I'm just trying to explain because you'll all be here someday, too.

One Tuesday, on a hot afternoon south of town where the Rock River elbows across the gravel, Mins de Boom was walking through the ditch grass when he came upon a case, black and square and of significant size. The scuff marks on its corners may have indicated it was thrown, like everything else, from a passing car. He had found things before that were valuable: a good jacket, a pair of boots, once or twice a wallet he'd returned forthwith, and enough t-shirts to fill a closet. But this was unusual.

He picked it up and ran his fingers along the leather, smudging out dirt marks, then dropped the bag of cans he'd already picked up and looked up at the road to see if anyone had seen him pick up what he'd discovered. When he saw no cars, he raised his knee and tried to open the case, but it was too big to open against his leg so he sat down and laid the case in front of him. There was no lock, only a pair of clasps that opened easily. When he raised the top, he was amazed to find, inside, a viola.

I think it was Elmer Janisse who spotted all this. Soon enough, there was a crowd. Now you might wonder how it is that a man like Mins de Boom even recognized this instrument as a viola: after all, most people in town wouldn't know a viola from a bass fiddle. The truth is Mins' mother played the viola in the old country, and played it often after her husband was taken away in those dark days of the war, on the nights when it was quiet and he and Lexie, the little Jewish girl they'd hid from the Nazis, sat in the kitchen to wait out the German occupation.

This viola was more orange-ish than the one he remembered his mother playing, but it was a viola nonetheless, tucked perfectly into the case's red felt. Two bows were clasped within the top of the case, along with a half-dozen extra strings in thin and square bags, and resin in the little compartment in the bottom, plus a strap of some type to wear over the shoulder.

He looked up once more and thought about his bicycle, back on the other side of the bridge, lying far enough down in the ditch not to be noticed by passers-by. The roar of cattle trucks on the highway not fifty feet away from his head nearly suffocated his daring, but once they had passed, he took out the viola and held it, warm, it seemed, with life, in his hands.

Actually, it had been lying in the sun since dawn.

It was, as are all great hand-crafted instruments, something of a miracle, light and shiny, the wood grain chevrons down its back translucent in the sun as he spun the instrument slowly in his hands. The ebony chin rest was scuffed with wear, like the fingerboard.

Inside the compartment with the resin, he'd seen a silver tuning fork, not unlike his mother's. With the neck of the viola in one hand, the bottom resting on his knee, he picked up the tuning fork and hit it lightly against the edge of the case, creating a tone so clear he thought it might have come from God.

He put down the fork and lifted the viola to his chin, curled his fingers around the unstained neck, and plucked the last string, the A-string, then reached up to the scroll and turned the peg slightly to measure the sound against the tone still singing in his ear.

Holding the viola in place, he closed the case once more with his right hand, then noted that the sun had not yet bleached the leather. It must have been there for no more than a day, at most, he thought.

It was, we think, the sheer pleasure of holding the instrument that made him feel suddenly guilty. He took hold of the handle of the case, held the viola in his right hand, and slid himself even deeper into the ditch to avoid being seen by the cars and trucks passing above him on the blacktop.

He reopened the case, laid the instrument down once more, then removed the top bow from its claps, tightened the horsehair as expertly as his mother had always done, retrieved the viola in his left hand, lifted it again to his chin, turned his neck to make its position comfortable, and slowly ran the bow over the A-string. It was glorious, and we use that word in ways you can only imagine. So many years had passed since he'd heard the throaty sound of even the instrument's highest string, that he was surprised to feel within himself some strange urgency he could identify only with the those dark nights of the Occupation, Lexie's eyes doleful, yet shining with hope.

Honestly, I have no trouble saying this – when you witness such things, it's a real joy to be dead.

By this time, with any foresight, you may well have guessed what was to happen at that spot, deep in the ditch beside Highway 75. We did, but we do have a leg up, so to speak. It is, of course, the miracle of this story, something of a miracle of life.

Mins de Boom sat in the ditch and played that viola, even though he had never had a lesson. Who knows what kind of Holy Spirit it was that occupied his instinct or passion to enable his fingers to locate the proper distances over the fingerboard? Was it a memory of his mother's playing in the shadowed candlelight as he stood beside her years ago? Was it something left unopened for almost fifty years?

Sometimes, even we don't understand how it is people do what they do, or how it is they come to keep their secrets. It's no wonder The Maker loves us.

Mins sat with his knees up against the slope and played an old psalm that came back to him as if it were perched forever in his memory. He played that psalm in his mother's old way, in a way she'd played them for Lexie, a way she thought Davidic, slow and relentless, each note something to be treasured and marked and encased in a glass box, the whole stanza creating a kind of Yiddish museum.

A lesser man would have cried, perhaps, to discover and, after so many years, to exercise such a gift in his fingers. A lesser man would have wept simply to remember those moments he had tried to lock away in his memory. But whatever quaking Mins de Boom may have felt within his soul or his heart was not shown so much on his face as it was felt in the tremor of the notes that rose from the strings of a viola someone had unknowingly dropped in the ditch on the way to Highland.

I know that it's taking me too long to tell this story, but Mins was a simple man, and the plain, low notes he lifted from the spirit of that instrument came very slowly, but not without passion. Have you ever really heard a Genevan Psalm? I'm not sorry for saying this, and I don't expect you to understand, but the melody is not for your world at all.

From the moment Mins de Boom put down the instrument that morning, he knew he could never again part with it, no matter what the circumstances. He brought it slowly to his knee and laid it carefully back in the case, then fixed the bow into the clasps at the top, snapped the button on the resin compartment, and laid the solitary piece of red felt cloth down perfectly over the bridge and strings, just as he'd found it. Then he closed the case securely and held it over his chest, as if there were no handle.

There we sat watching, a couple dozen of us at least. Honestly, you don't know what you're missing.

Anyway, country ditches today are full of plastic. Large sheets of black plastic rip away from silage covers on farms all over this county and blow in the stiff prairie winds, then catch on barbed wire, where they hang like black flags until the wind itself shreds them into pieces that eventually blow away forever.

Mins found a broad shard of black plastic and wound the case inside, then carried it under his arm in the bottom of the ditch, all the way to the bridge, where his bicycle lay. He knew that some of the passersby might recognize that he'd found something unusual, since on ordinary days the twin baskets over the back tire of his bicycle flashed with cans and bottles, so he lowered the dark treasure carefully into one of those rear baskets after dumping the cans he'd earlier picked up into the basket on the other side. Forgetting the rest of the ditch for that day, he pedaled back into town.

Some people noticed his homecoming that morning, not because of the black bundle in his basket, but because of the way he kept his face down beneath the brim of that second-hand Panama that Lena had bought him, as if he were fighting a terrifying northwest wind or driving rain. Of course, Mins wanted no one to recognize his triumphal entry.

But if there's one thing Mins is not, it's invisible. After all those years as the school janitor, he knew most of the people in town – and most knew him. But then, trust me on this, no single human being ever really knows another. Who in the village of Highland would have guessed that Mins de Boom could play the viola? Perhaps the greatest mystery of all is how much you don't know about each other.

When he came home, he unwrapped the case from the black plastic and stood it in the garage. Lena was out hanging clothes. She came in when it was standing there, unwrapped, on the work bench. For her, he drew the viola carefully from the case and showed it to her, holding the instrument in two hands, as if it were an offering.

"Whose is it?" she asked.

He told her where he'd found it.

"It must be worth something," she told him. "You should advertise." Mins nodded, but, as you might expect, he didn't intend to.

The next day she came out to the garage and saw it there yet, and she reminded him that it would only be right to get it back to its owner.

She told him he could call in to the radio, to Swap Shop. "There may be a reward," she told him. "Besides," she said, "if no one answers the ad, we can sell it ourselves."

Mins knew all of that to be true.

Now you may ask yourself why he didn't play that viola for Lena right then and there. We understand that question. But let me just say that some things are better left a mystery, sometimes even to us. We think he may have guessed it would shock her to know he could play the way he could. Maybe he feared this fragile balance of their relationship would be threatened by her knowing his secret. On the other hand, perhaps the memory was so deeply secured within him that it couldn't emerge in the presence of another human being in this foreign country. It's perfectly human to want to know – we all understand that – but it's perfectly divine simply to enjoy. That, you still must learn.

Three days later, when the two of them drove the car into the garage after church on a Sunday morning, she saw that viola standing there. "Surely you don't mean to keep it?" she asked him. "It must be valuable."

"Oh, no – no, no, no," Mins told her. "This week I will for sure put an ad in the *Shopper*."

Now the whole town knew that if something was lost in the ditches outside of town, Mins de Boom would see it. Perhaps he himself might have found it. And once the Straaks family determined that their daughter's viola had inadvertently fallen from their van one night in an emergency, Mr. Straaks called Mins de Boom.

"Mins," he said, his voice booming over the phone, "my daughter somehow lost her viola.

We think maybe it went in the ditch up from the Highland corner somewhere." Mins's ears burned.

"You didn't spot it, did you?"

He heard his wife pick up another phone in the basement.

"It had to be the only lost viola in the ditch south of town," Mr. Straaks joked.

Mins, being Mins, had no choice – not only because Lena was listening, either. The man couldn't lie deftly about such things; in fact, he couldn't really lie at all.

"You should see my daughter," Mr. Straaks said. "She's absolutely heartbroken. Not to mention the fact that it wasn't exactly cheap."

"This viola," he asked, "it's orange-ish?"

"Yes," Mr. Straaks said. "Yes, of course that's the one. I'm sure."

He waited, maybe ten seconds, agonizing seconds, I'm sure. "It's here," he said, "in my garage."

"Oh, thank God," Mr. Straaks said. "Listen, I can't get over there anymore tonight, but first thing in the morning, all right? First thing in the morning, I'll send my daughter over – she'll be so relieved."

Lena never said a word. To her, the viola was a very lucky find. She hoped that Straaks, whom she knew because of the tall pillars on their beautiful new home across town, would give them a generous reward.

That night, late, when Lena was already asleep, Mins got a strange notion into his mind, something that got him up and out of his bed and made him leave the bedroom across from hers. It was, of course, the viola. He lit a candle he kept on the workbench in the garage, and lifted the instrument out of its case with the same care he had that first morning he'd found it. Then he looked back at the door to the house. He undid a bow, and waited there like a soloist for a nod from the maestro, the neck of the instrument in his left hand. He walked back to the door and opened it, listened for any noise at all. By the light of the candle, he could see the time on the old classroom clock he'd hung above the workbench. It was after two.

What he felt was the naked desire to have that delicate instrument make its music, for he didn't think of what he'd felt that morning in the ditch as *his* playing really, never considered that what beauty emerged from that viola had in fact been prompted by anything within his janitor's soul. The music was, to him, as so much was, simply something as divine as sunshine, something even a bit of sin to deny once more. He looked around him, at the faint shadows dancing off the slate walls of the garage, but determined the garage was not the place for the music that he knew would come again.

He was afraid to start the car, afraid to raise the mechanical garage door he had recently installed, so he had no choice. He put the viola back in the case and steered that Dutch bike out of the garage to steal away quietly, that viola wrapped in his bathrobe. He pulled on a jersey and his bibs, stepped into his clogs and walked the bike, the case in the basket, down the driveway to the street and toward the place that seemed suddenly God-sent, the Highland Cemetery.

He didn't pedal quickly – Lena sleeps heavily, he knew. And when he got here he saw the dampness shine on the grass in the moon's bright glow, took off his clogs as if he were back at home in his mother's house, and walked barefoot into the stones at the edge the south end, to the place where the town, years ago, had buried children who'd died unexpectedly, quite a distance from any house in the neighborhood.

And there Mins de Boom played that viola once more, the last time he would ever touch that instrument, or any like it, in his lifetime. There he wrapped his clean fingers gently around the unstained neck and brought the bow softly to the strings again, calling up music his mother had played so many years before, music he'd heard sometimes when hidden away in that storage space while waiting for the Nazis to climb back into their vehicles, his entire repertoire only those same hymns and psalms, having absolutely no idea of the number of saints right there beside him to savor the only divine recital he'd ever offer the world.

A mercury-vapor lamp stands over the wrought iron of the gate up here in the graveyard. Late at night, sitting there looking over the forest of graves, someone could easily imagine that the glints and shimmering echoes on the gravestones were only reflections of that big light up behind him, that lamp high up over the gate.

But if you had been there that night, if you had seen Mins holding that viola, barefooted and bath-robed, and listened to his divine music, seen him sitting up against a stone playing something in his soul I'm not sure even he understood, you may well have thought, as he did himself, that those lights all around were the shining eyes of schoolchildren sitting respectfully for a guest concert by an accomplished European master, playing for God.

You would have been wrong, of course, as he was, but there are times, trust me, when pure delusion is pure blessing.

The next day, little Sylvia Straaks came by happily to retrieve her viola. Mins stood with a stubborn smile and handed it to her, noting especially the joy and relief on the child's face.

So no single man or woman from Highland ever heard Mins de Boom play the viola that somehow had come to him as a gift, albeit for such a short time. We believe he'll be up here soon, his body now wracked by cancer. Perhaps, as the school board said, he should have stopped rolling his own cigarettes.

It will comfort you to know that when it happens, Lena will attend him faithfully in those hours as he approaches his death, in the stable way he long ago approached his Lord.

When he comes, I'm sure it will take some time for him to wander out. He has never been particularly forward. We have already decided that that night – and we know well enough to say it will be night when he arrives – we'll meet him with just a few of us from his church. He is, after all, the kind of man who may be surprised at who's here.

But we all so loved his playing that night, his music of the spheres, that we have taken care to get for him something that will please him, a special gift in a special case, which he will open, or so we believe, with the delighted shining eyes of a child.

And then once more, he will play for all of us and all the stars and all the planets above.

Phoenix

From the moment Ike Fortuin arrived up here, he was a man on a mission. Once he got his bearings, he marched over to his grandma's stone, expecting her to step out of the grave to greet him and answer the question he'd wanted to ask her for most of his life.

She didn't. She was out.

When he was a boy, he'd accidentally walked in on her death. He'd been downtown and on his way home; it was early evening, and he'd simply stopped at her place, as he'd done often for goodies. That wasn't unusual.

The thing is, she'd just then suffered a major heart attack – the visitation, little Ike discovered later that night, of the dreaded old man we used to call the Grim Reaper. She'd been in bed when her heart went south, and his Uncle Wiley, who happened to be there, was sitting beside her when Ike walked in.

In the middle of some panting and shrieking he'd never forgotten, she looked up at the wall on the other side of the room and said, "Wiley, please, please, please, turn that picture around." They were, to him, his grandma's dying words.

When Uncle Wiley turned to see the picture, he saw his nephew standing there innocently. No one knows why, exactly, but Ike's being there seemed to anger Wiley so greatly that he grabbed his nephew's little arm and ushered him out of the house. Ike never knew if Uncle Wiley had turned that framed photograph around as Grandma had demanded, and never even knew whose picture it was. What he didn't forget was that, before or after, Uncle Wiley had never spoken to him quite like that, as if what was happening in the room was somehow shameful.

But he'd always remembered his grandma's odd request to turn that framed picture around, a picture that someone – Uncle Wiley himself? – must have removed because it wasn't there when Ike went back a couple days later, after the funeral. What photograph was held in that frame? – that's what he wanted to know, that's what he wanted to ask his grandma, and that's what he'd told his wife obsessively in those not-infrequent episodes when she needed Kleenex to get him through.

Ike Fortuin had those kinds of nights.

He'd come back from Vietnam riddled with horrors he rarely talked about and none of us knew much about nor took the time to ask. Post-Traumatic Stress Disorder is the kind of chronic condition, like drink, that a hard-working town like Highland doesn't countenance well.

But then, truth be told, Ike never was an easy man to like, which is not to say people hated him. Long before he'd returned from Vietnam, Ike Fortuin on your back porch was no better than a swarm of black flies. Vietnam only made things worse, it seemed. Nobody knew a thing, he wouldn't talk about it, and other vets shrugged their shoulders and claimed that what he'd seen was nothing near the worst of it.

But it was downright strange for a rookie to get up like a man possessed and march off to another stone, as if death weren't so much an end as an errand. It took no coaxing to get him up and going. He just stepped out of the coffin and proceeded to lay siege to his grandma's place.

Now you shouldn't think of us as county fair midway targets, popping up as if spring-loaded from our vaults. We don't, and we're not. Besides, that we're redeemed doesn't mean we're fashioned by a divine cookie-cutter. We're all a little different, variety being the spice of life *and* death. Some of us only rarely show ourselves, and others, preternaturally social, would drive the rest of us loony if we weren't, post mortem, hardwired to love. Just look around sometime.

You'll see differences all over the place. Some last.

Then again, some of us aren't here. Highland Cemetery isn't a mental ward. While we can't slip back into what you call life, some of us take vacations to die for, you might say. Some folks visit other neighborhoods for years, lifetimes, which is really saying the same thing, come to think of it. Being ghostly has startling benefits, time-wise.

What I'm saying is, the night Ike wanted to see his grandma, Trudy Fortuin simply didn't appear to be around.

"I just assumed she'd be here," he said to me when she didn't show up. "Waiting for you?" I asked.

He looked stupefied, and let down.

"I haven't seen her in a while," I told him. "I think she's in France again."

He was stunned. "They allow that?" he asked me.

"*Allow?*" I said. If there's anything hard to take once you're gone, it's a precocious newbie know-it-all. "You mean *allowing* her to see other men?" I said.

Ike's grandfather is here, but he and Trudy aren't close – civil, but not close, and they hadn't been for years before they each made the trek up the hill alone. We're reconditioned, you might say, but not reupholstered.

"Oh, I know about Brethhower," he told me. "I know the story."

"He comes by every once in a while himself," I told him, " – not the only guy in uniform."

"He died there, in France," he said, as if I needed to be enlightened. "That's right – you used to edit the paper. You used to know everything."

I shrugged my shoulders. "Not as much as I know now," I told him.

"Is that healthy?" he asked.

"Health isn't an issue," I told him.

"Geez," he said, "just think of the writer you'd be if you knew it all back then."

"Trust me – it would have been a burden."

That stopped him, or maybe it was the fact that, just as we were speaking, his grandma Trudy simply showed up on the arm of Cpl. Henry Brethhower, in full dress uniform, the two of them undeniably youthful.

What Ike wasn't prepared for was a 1940-ish grandma, her long curls splendidly up top her head in a bundle of victory rolls. She looked, as some might say, divine, and she greeted him by curling her hand around his neck, as if he were still the lad he was when she last saw him, a sweet and warm gesture, and odd since it seemed she was dressed as if she could have been his granddaughter.

But Grandma Trudy knew very well what he was after. "It was a picture of *my* grandma," she told Ike without having to be asked. "It was a picture of my old grandmother with her two children," she told him, "the only one I had of her – tintype. I just couldn't look at it."

Ike seemed nervous, but then he always did, even when he wasn't dead.

"That's what you wanted to know, isn't it?" Grandma Trudy asked, smiling. "On the night I died, you heard me tell Wiley that I wanted that picture turned around, the picture of my grandma with my mom and Oom Baas.

Ike was, at that moment, considerably premature in terms of settling in. We *are* different. He pointed with his right hand, then waved as if he were cleaning a window between him and that WWII pair not five feet from where he stood. "Can you do that?" he said, finally.

"Do what?" Trudy said.

"Can you just choose how old you want to be?" Just like that, he looked down at himself, in sport coat and tie, as if he expected shorts and a t-shirt.

"Takes some little getting used to," Brethhower said. "Seems so unnatural, I suppose." "But that's it, isn't it?" Grandma Trudy asked him. "That's what you've been dying to know?"

It's an old joke, but Ike was too stunned to catch it. "Where's Grandpa?" he asked. "Around somewhere, I'm sure," she told him. Without taking her arm out of Henry's, she took a look around the cemetery, then shook her head. "He could be anywhere, I guess." "He's not with you?"

"Maybe I should introduce myself," Henry said, a shade embarrassed maybe. "My name is Henry Breth –"

"I know – I know," Ike told him. "You died on June 6, 1944 – on Omaha Beach."

Brethhower tipped his head.

"I'm shocked to see you together," Ike said. "I shouldn't be, I suppose." "Perfectly understandable," Brethhower told him. "No need to apologize."

For a moment, an earthly, awkward silence grew up all around, something I hadn't experienced for quite some time, but Ike was still ascending the eternal learning curve and he needed some soak time. He seemed not to have shed that irritating fidgeting, but then he'd just arrived.

Grandma Trudy finally pulled away from Henry and stood there directly before Ike, then took his arms in her hands, slid them down to his, and held them ceremoniously before finally taking him fully in a sweet and polite hug.

Ike Fortuin, befuddled, had never been a man people would choose to hug. He'd spent most his life mulling mysteries he wanted solved the moment he'd die, and when finally he did, the answer felt somehow insubstantial, coming as it did from a woman in a pea coat with pointy shoulders, a feathery hat over her curls, a woman arm-in-arm with a war hero he'd never seen. She said it the moment she met him: what had been there on the bedroom wall was a picture of her own grandma and her two kids.

"You're probably wondering *why*, too," Grandma Trudy said finally. "It's what you wanted to know, Ike, but I assume what you really wanted was to know was why." She turned back to Cpl. Brethhower and gave him a signal they'd settled on before so that he moved aside a bit, in a gentlemanly way, and just like that a very old woman appeared from the dark in a black dress and a black hat complete with hairnet, an old wrinkled, toothless woman who looked as if she'd just come from grave. (We can say things like that and not risk offense.)

"Let me just 'vonce look at you," that old woman said in a thick Dutch brogue, and she walked up to Ike and looked him over in a way I remember movies showing Native people, oddly charmed, staring at a paleface for the first time.

She pointed at her face, then at his. "You have my father's proud forehead, but not his hair," she told him.

"Your father?" Ike asked.

"He died on the ship," she told him.

We still see through a glass darkly, after a fashion. I mean, what we see and know is so much more than what we once did that you can't think of us as if we were simply placed in some parallel universe. But there are things about the Peloponnesian Wars I don't know, things about the Ice Age, about Shoeless Joe or the Australian Outback. I could get there faster than Google, but the truth is I had only the foggiest notion of who this old woman was or what she was talking about. There are still some fairly substantial learning curves on our highways, too.

Trudy looked at her grandson. "I knew he died on the ship, the *Phoenix*," she told him, and then turned to her grandmother, "but I never knew the story, Oma."

It's not always easy to tell where light comes from these days up the hill, but the longer this Oma of hers was with us, the brighter her face shown. I swear it. Maybe it was just my eyes acclimating.

"*Ach*, Trudy always wanted to know the story of the ship, in't so?" Oma said and smiled, warmly. "I never once told a soul," she said, "not even my man." A breath away stood an even older man sporting a perfectly silver beard the width of a paint brush.

I don't always understand divine technology, so I'm not sure how it was that I myself got the trip that wondrously transpired just then. Oma Fortuin had been there – she earned a spot on whatever supersonic vehicle winged us back a century and a half; and Grandma Trudy was part of the whole story that fidgety Ike, himself an old guy, had waited so long to hear. All of that made sense. But how it was that Joanie and I got a ride, I'll never quite understand. The old Dutchman with the silver goatee went along, too, as did Cpl. Henry B. and who-knows-how- many others in the cloud that swarmed behind like the tail of a whirlwind.

In the twinkling of an eye we were shivering on a broad, sandy beach in late November, a place I know I'd never visited. Not shivering really, either; if I weren't entirely dead, I would have been shivering because something in me wanted badly to shake. Standing out there on the lakeshore that early winter night was deathly cold. A fire was raging on the beach, and another was lit far enough out on the lake to create an eerie auburn dome that shimmered in the inky darkness.

"It was November – I will tell you now – November of 1847," Oma said, but the years had disappeared, her face shining radiantly, her hair rearranging itself into pipe curls as if just behind her stood an accomplished stylist at work in dreamy silence.

Ike seemed nervous to me, as if she were about to tell his story. That would have been something.

"We left Varssevelt," she told us. "The farm was no good. Men were arrested when they worshipped. The new country seemed a dream. My father's eyes – I can see them now – they were bright when he spoke of America. How they still shine." She pointed up at the man behind her. "He was a good man."

"The truth?" Ike asked. "Your father?"

Look, it's not something that happens every day – six generations stood on that beach, if my fingers didn't lie. And we were there, too, plus more than a few noseys from up the hill. It had become a community thing.

Oma smiled, as if all of this made sense. "We sailed from Holland to New York. Then by train to Buffalo," she told us, looking out over the beach, where a couple dozen people were huddling over the big fire, all of them looking out over the water.

"We left Buffalo, I think it was eleven, November… Thursday – to here, Gertrude. We were coming here." She spoke as if to the sand beneath our feet. "We had come so far, *ja?* – so far." She squinted, harshly. "And we were so close. All the way from Holland," she said. "We were so close."

The lake lay black as pitch, the night moonless. "Watch now." She pointed east.

Ike's face, I swear, was jittery, alive. This whole thing was for him, all of this.

"We stopped in Manitowoc. The lake was high and rough. The captain said we would stay in the harbor until it was safe."

I'm telling you, she'd become the girl she'd been way back then.

"Some people cried, I remember. Some even swore about that captain – we were so close, you know."

Cpl. Brethhower kept his arm around Grandma Fortuin, his betrothed. He died on just such a beach. Had to be memories.

The old man with the beard spoke. "I stayed up that night with many men." His daughter took his hand. "None of us could sleep," he told us. "It was the last night, and we had come all the way from Holland."

Oma was still looking out over the water. "I dreamed, too – dry land, a house, a sunny sky." She glanced back at her father, still holding his hand. "Our ship left harbor late. I was only a little girl. I was sleeping, dreaming of the house. But Vader stood on the deck, watching shore lights – and then I remember him standing over me. He woke me. He woke all of us. He spoke softly. '*Opstaan*, Mina!' he said."

The old man stared into the darkness, nodding.

"We all knew." She looked back at Trudy as if what she was to say was not to be missed. "His eyes blazed like the fire." She raised a hand to her ears. "I remember it all very well, for in my whole life I saw him never again." She leaned into her father's side just as she might have when she was a girl.

Not far away, a man was picking up driftwood to feed the fire on the beach.

"The hold was full of Hollanders. Many more than was right," Oma said. "In a moment, everyone was awake – men yelled and children screamed and Mother gathered us quickly in our night clothes. She didn't reach for any of her things. We hurried up on the deck. I remember going up the ladder. Emma pushed me up. We were almost the first."

It was 1847, November of 1847, a Lake Michigan beach.

"Smoke was in the air, Gertrude," Oma said. "Mother pushed us – she carried me to the side of the ship, made us sit and kneel, then sat beside us and pointed to shore. She spoke, in Dutch.

'*Kijk.*' She pointed, '*daar is ons huis.*'" Behind us people were screaming, but Mother kept us at the rail – she made us watch lights on the shore. We were so close. Do you understand? We were so very close to home."

There we stood, all of us.

"Emma asked her about father – she said he would be here soon. She said he is fighting the fire. Mama watched for him – I saw her. There was fear in her eyes. I was just a little girl, but I saw it. I knew." Oma seemed almost to bow. "Then there was an explosion." She looked at her granddaughter – and then Ike, too. She didn't forget Ike. Then back at Trudy. "I should have told you, maybe," she said. "You were so young. But there is yet more."

Her father helped her. "The explosion blew up the middle of the ship," he said calmly, as if he'd been over this a hundred times.

"Fire went shooting up behind us," Oma said. "It made my back so hot. But the air was cold – November, the twenty-first, Sunday morning – *ja*, that's something, the Sabbath, the Lord's Day." Her smile was surprising, but not strange. We *are* different. "Mother pushed us tighter against the rail. There was much shouting – no, screaming. People ran like animals. They just had on nightclothes. And the fire grew. It was so hot. I cried. We all did."

She was there on the beach, too – her mother. The circle just kept growing, the rest of us silent as Catechism.

"Wooden shoes banged on the deck. Men shouted and screamed. Mother understood no English. Some women went crazy, Gertrude – they screamed so hard I couldn't stand it. Some laughed like witches. And everywhere there were children, Dutch children, my friends, lost from mothers and fathers. It was terrible."

Ike stood speechless, but all of us were. It was, I think, one of the few moments of his life when he wasn't filling the air with nervous talk. When Oma began to wipe tears from her face, she'd become a little girl.

"There was an American – a good man, like my father. He was handsome. A rich man. He played with us often on the ship. His name was Mr. Blish. He was there, suddenly, by mother.

"*Vrouw*,' he said, 'your man?'" Then Oma Fortuin looked up at her mother for the first time, who nodded as if to say that what lay before them was hallowed ground.

"Mother made us all hold hands. It was hard to walk – to stay together. People rushed all around us. I saw a woman with only a wool skirt on. She jumped over the side of the ship, screaming. Mr. Blish led us through. I had hold of mother's hand. She squeezed it so tight. I cried. I can feel it yet, after these many years."

Everything came quickly now, the crowd still gathering.

"The flames grew behind us. You could hear the loud snapping noise. Then Mr. Blish stopped. 'Here,' he said – but Emma – she was the oldest – Emma was gone."

But then she was there, too, another child, Emma, a reunion.

"Mother screamed out her name, but she was gone." The two of them held hands.

"Mr. Blish grabbed my mother's arms and shook her. I remember hating him for that. I tried to kick him, to make him stop hurting her. He picked me up, above his head, held me there. He pushed through the crowd. In a moment I was in a boat. There was a strange lady next to me. She took me in her arms. Suddenly I was cold, so cold. The boat was in the lake, away from the flames."

Oma Fortuin was the only one of her family to escape death that night of the burning ship. They were all there behind her, beside her, but only she had lived.

"I was alone. I was just a little girl, and I was alone. I cried for my mother." "You weren't alone," her mother said.

"I pounded on the strange woman's breast. She held me still tighter. *Wees still, kleintje*,' she said."

Ike Fortuin stood just outside the circle of immigrants, lost in a story he'd never heard, a story of his own family. You learn a lot, dying.

"The boat was filled with people," Oma said, pointing to the dark horizon where a rescue boat had just then appeared. "We could hold no more. Water was coming in." She drew the collar of her dress up as if she were cold. "Some men used wooden shoes to scoop it. A woman came up from the water and pulled herself up. Her eyes were big. But we could hold no more and a man pushed her away. She held to the side. I remember seeing the hand. Then, it was gone. My feet were in the water. It was so cold."

We were, just then, all of us, survivors.

"I can still see the ship, Gertrude. It is so clear in my mind – look there." We couldn't help but raise our eyes. "The fire flew high from the water. So high. Another explosion. I saw bodies in the air. I saw them splash into the water. The flames were louder than the screaming, but I heard Dutch words, American words. Prayers. Curses. It was – I thought of this often – it was something of Hell."

Ike was lost, I swear it. He was gone, not literally, but lost in the story. His Grandma Trudy was standing there in the arms of a man she once loved, who was, I think, somewhere on his own beach just then. We were all there, and none of us was.

"Finally, we came to shore," Oma said.

And there was the lifeboat all right, and in a moment we all stood around the fire that had seemed half a beach away.

"Someone started a fire to warm us," she said. "I was so cold. The frost made the beach hard like clay. It was November, late in November – a Sunday, a Sabbath morning."

I didn't have to ask, but I was afraid of where Ike Fortuin had gone in all of this. "Did you know?" I asked him. He'd just arrived, after all, just that late afternoon.

"I was afraid to die," Grandma Trudy told him, looked up at Ike, her grandson. "That night you stopped by my house and found me in bed, the last night of my life – I was afraid to die."

That, too, didn't need to be said. We all were.

"She alone survived – my Oma Fortuin," Trudy said, pointing at the little girl with the blanket wrapped tightly around her, her own grandma. "She'd lost everyone else – all of her family when that immigrant ship burned and sank, and I couldn't look at her just then – I couldn't. It was too much pain. Do you understand, Ike?"

"For all those years," Oma said. "For all those many years of my life, I could never get out of my mind why it should happen that way, all of my family, gone." There she sat, a child maybe, her whole loving family around her. "For all of my life, I wanted to know why, I wanted to hear it from the Lord God himself." There they were, together in each other's arms on the same cold beach.

And at that moment with my own eyes I saw what had happened to Ike Fortuin, how a buddy, a fellow grunt, had died ever so slowly just on the other side of an embankment that suddenly rose right there on the beach that became a rice patty, a dark-haired kid who'd been carrying a radio when six or eight of them walked into a firefight; how the radio man was hit hard and bad and fell on the other side of that steep embankment, his radio still squawking like something alive, a beleaguered voice begging directions, begging a response, and how Ike, just on the other side of that embankment, a blaze of gunfire all around him, absolutely could not get to his feet and cross that embankment and help his fallen buddy because he was sure that if he would even get to his knees, he too would die; and always that radio full of screaming voices on the other side, alarms and just noise – I heard all of that myself – those voices screaming for compass points, for some answer from someone, and Ike Fortuin, just a kid, splayed out on the ground on the other side of all that gunfire, tears in his eyes, and all that squawking going on and him knowing his friend was dying not twenty feet away and he somehow absolutely powerless to get to his feet and save him, his good, good buddy, his friend, bleeding to death, and he himself unmoving for what seemed just a few days later to be forever.

And I knew – we all did – what came back to Ike Fortuin on too many nights after that was that god-awful shrieking from the radio, all those rounds of paralyzing gunfire, and the death-like touch of wet grass seeping into his fatigues, imprisoned in the profound and unforgiveable fear that kept him from doing what he had to do, what he wanted to, what he should have done.

Should have done.

"I wanted to know why," Oma said, surrounded by her family. "For so many years, I wanted to know why so many of my people, my family had to die. For so many years, I wanted to get here because then maybe I would know." She stopped, looked up at her father. "And when I did, I found you," she told her family, and Ike, and Grandma Trudy, who already knew.

And then I swear even he was there, the radio man, in full gear, even the helmet, which he took off and placed under his arm. Cpl. Brethhower saluted, and Ike Fortuin stood motionless, incapable of moving anything until that young kid in uniform walked up to him and put his arm around Ike's neck right there on the beach in front of us all.

Ike Fortuin had marched right up to his grandma's grave, as if on a mission, I think I said, but what happened that night brought him fully into the world of the dead – and the redeemed.

It's not a story I could have told back in town. It's not a story I could have written. Who would buy it? It's a story only some of us, I suppose, can believe.

There was Oma, surrounded by the family she'd lost in a cold lake in November of 1847; and Grandma Trudy, in the arms of the man whom she'd lost on Omaha Beach for almost a century; and fidgety Ike Fortuin, his thin arms growing back their musculature around a kid, a buddy he may well have let die somewhere, long ago, in a rice patty he could never fully leave.

If this isn't Heaven, I don't know what is.

January Thaw

She was a Brink, and the Brinks were timid by nature. Soon enough, she'd heard how some of us had walked over to look at where they'd buried him, gawking as if his being there was some freak show. Made her laugh to think about it, but then people had always been afraid of him. Really, in some ways, we were really waiting *for her* to meet him, wondering what might be said.

At first, he was sitting against a fencepost – his stone wasn't up yet – those long legs stretched out before him as he looked out west and north. It seemed as if, since his arrival, he'd rather enjoyed being alone, far in the corner, staring into the open fields. Not angry, either, but looking over the land as if it was a place to which he'd always wanted to return.

No one spoke to him. But then, he had a certain reputation.

Up here there are others with reputations, too, but not quite like his.

Occasionally, that first week or so, the rest of us felt awkward around her because we didn't know how she would feel about his being there, this man, given what he'd done to her.

So the Brinks being who they are, and he being who he was, we think Jennie just waited a while, with the patience of someone in glory. He was such a presence, always was. And he was big. He was a man. Even when he was an old man, he was a man – huge, rangy shoulders.

The first few times she dropped by – her place was a couple hundred feet or so from his, not far – she kept herself hidden behind those big stones just south of his because she simply wanted to see him, those long legs, that great white shock of hair, a shard of big blue stem jutting from his mouth, something he'd pulled from the fence line. Sometimes, he'd stare down the hill toward the town, the grain elevator, the bridge, and the river. And she saw it, too, what we had said about his being almost oblivious to the rest of us – not surprisingly – but we all saw how he smiled, as if he'd made the right choice when he picked out this spot, as if something down there was special to him, something she thought she understood, maybe even better than others.

Not everyone is as happy as he was. Sometimes it takes a while – not long – before the angry ones get settled down and neighborly. Then again, some never do. They just stay in the ground or disappear altogether, which is sad.

We were all sure he would have chosen to live if he'd had the choice, even though he was as old as he was, as old as most of the people in the neighborhood, many of whom were actually happy to get here, finally, comforted, their agony behind them, some of them claiming – somewhat jokingly – that they'd already been to Hell. When she hears such things, sometimes – not all the time, but sometimes – she's less grieved about having found herself here as young as she was at the time, just 21 years old, and leaving her baby, her first, behind. That's another story.

Sometime that first month, I asked her whether or not she'd struck up a conversation with him yet. Like I said, we waited, too, all of us. We just left him alone a while.

"Has anyone?" she asked me, somewhat perturbed.

I shrugged my shoulders. "We're wondering about you – that's all."

She looked away as the Brinks often do.

Time is irrelevant, of course, but it took a while before she came out from behind the Stravers' family stone just south of his, and by then it was cold, and she had to pull her coat around her, that old blue one, double-breasted, the one her mother had given her so many years ago for a wedding present.

In life, I may have known him best, one of his few admirers in Highland. I had all his books, every one of them signed personally to me. My sister has them now. She could have sold them for a bundle, but she kept them because of how much I loved them, I think. For a long time, he was what I wished I was, a novelist.

Anyway, I'm guessing that when he spotted Jennie he smiled because she was the kind of tall, willowy young woman that had always pleased him, his dream, as were so many of his women, the ones in his novels.

When she came to him from the darkness, the collar of that thick blue coat pulled up around her face, it seemed he didn't recognize her. Some of us watched – not everyone – and what we saw that first time they noticed each other is that nothing happened at all. He glanced up, then fell back into that pleased stare he wore as he looked over the snow fields north and east.

She went back to her place to redesign what she imagined she would say because it had not dawned on her – his knowing as much about her as he did, so very much – that he *wouldn't* know her, wouldn't even recognize her. But then, he hadn't been around town for so many years. As if that should matter. She had to laugh when she thought of it because, of course, neither had she.

He was an old man when he died, and she was quite young when she passed, even though he'd been just a boy when she was in her agony. Back then, she barely knew him, not even in his teens. But still, when she walked over to meet him there in the neighborhood, she couldn't miss the fact he still had some youthfulness. She'd felt it the moment he'd looked at her that first time. She is a woman, and even though she died so very young, she had learned – as women do – to read men's eyes. Nothing was said, but I wondered if after that first time in the short silence, she had considered not returning, afraid of him in a way that mostly we aren't up here, but as, I suppose, she had cause to be.

So she waited, maybe, for a January thaw, a cold, crisp night with an incandescent moon that shone on the faces of the stones and cast shadows across the thin carpet of snow, a night when her going to him cast the whole place into silence because we still wondered what she thought of him, the man who had claimed to know so much more than he should about her – as if he'd seen her naked, as if he'd actually watched her make love with the man who would become her husband – who's not here, by the way. The Depression took him to California and, unlike the writer, he never returned.

I like to think she went to him that night, late, thinking maybe she'd be most alone. It was cold, but not forbidding, that blue coat wrapped tightly around her, collar up. She wanted to think her meeting with him a secret almost, but she knows better. The rest of us are all around.

You need to see it this way – he is leaning up against his own stone, a leather coat with a sheepskin collar pulled up against a light northwest wind. He is twice her size.

"You don't know me?" she said.

He smiles. He always loved the attention of young and beautiful women. "Is that a question?" he answers.

She probably hadn't expected another question, and it was intimidating this first time to be in his presence. "You scare me," she tells him, which is something no one would expect a Brink to say, but up here, fear, for the most part, has been gratefully left behind.

Always genial, he tries to diffuse her tentativeness. "We're both long gone," he says, jokingly. "Besides, you're young enough to be my daughter."

"I'm old enough to be your mother," she says.

"Vander Es – you have high cheekbones like a Vander Es." He points that long finger. "Somewhere in your family line there's Indian blood."

She shakes her head.

"Brandsma?" he says. "Tall women, all of them. Good strong Frisian stock."

That he could be that wrong makes her smile. "Van Engen," she tells him.

His eyes narrow, his shoulders hunch just a bit, just a second or two before a long knowing smile – something she doesn't like – spreads across his face in slow motion. He says nothing.

She nods, because she knows at that moment that he does. "And where is it – this secret place?" she says. Deliberately, she turns her back to him, walks just a few steps north, almost to the fence. "I could look forever – I have," she says, insistent. "There is no 'secret place' out here. This year, beans; the next year, corn – that's all. There is no 'Garden of Eden,' as you called it. Long, flat land – very beautiful. But no secret place. You couldn't have brought some girl here yourself because there isn't such a place."

She turns back to him when he offers her no answer. With his finger, he taps his temple three times.

"You can simply lie like that, and we have no say in it?" she says. "I mean, those people you've lied about – we have no recourse?"

He stands, not to make her cower, but he may be thinking that there is disrespect in the way he's slouching, and he wants her to know that what she's said – about lying – does matter.

"I wasn't using you," he tells her.

"Then who were you using?" she asks him.

"I mean, I wasn't using *you*. I wasn't using the real you." He steps toward her as if to touch her with some comfort; he's not unfeeling. But she turns away with enough clarity to let him know that she'll have nothing of that. In life, I'm not sure he could have read that gesture, but he's dead now, and smarter, less imprisoned, you might say. He laughs, not at her – he laughs because he's always thought he had a way with women – more than what he did at least. He holds his hands up as if to come clean. "No reason to be afraid. I'm not my characters," he says.

"And I'm here to say that neither are we," she tells him, the collar from her coat falling back as she looks coldly over her shoulder. She waits. Waiting comes easily to all of us because we have no reason to hurry. She looks away again, this time over the valley toward the east.

The cemetery lies a mile or so west of town, up on a bluff above the river. The view is wonderful, the town down there beneath us, streetlights like a string of pearls in the midnight darkness, now and then a car. Occasionally, one of them comes up the road, driving west. The tires sing a higher pitch as they cross the bridge, but most of the time – everyone remembers the exceptions – those cars just keep going, especially at night. No one in our neighborhood hides as they pass, but then no one is afraid. Why should we be? From the road, there's nothing to see.

But Jennie knows she needs more from him. "What makes you think you know what happened – between Garrett and me, I mean?" she asks. She turns to face him, not because she'd planned it that way, but because now she wants him to answer her, not evade. "What makes you think you can create all of that out of thin air and sell it as your own?"

"You don't understand –"

"It wasn't 'thin air' either," she tells him. "Believe me, I wouldn't feel the way I do if it was all 'thin air,'" she says, but she's not angry.

"I didn't even know you," he tells her.

"Then how is it you think you can become me the way you did?"

"'Become you?'"

"Tell the whole world what happened to me – to us – here, in this 'secret place' that doesn't even exist." She pointed north and west. "Walk with me, why don't you?" she says. "Let me show you."

"You don't have to –"

"Let's go to this 'Garden of Eden,'" she insists. "Let's find this place you describe where he took me, this secret place where Garrett and I first made love." She comes up close to him, and even though he stands a foot taller than she does, she is, believe me, unafraid. "You're surprised that I say it that way?" She looks into his eyes. "Why? I was as human as you. Maybe that's why it hurt –"

"When I wrote that book," he says, "you were already gone."

"Not so," she says, raising a hand as if it were self-evident. "I was here." "If I'd have known –"

"If you'd have known, it wouldn't have stopped you for a moment," she tells him, her voice astoundingly mellow, restrained. "You were driven. It was your calling – these stories. It was what you were born to do, you said." And now she takes hold of him at the elbow. "Let's go – you and me – let's go find this secret place."

"I made it up," he says. "You know that."

"But you didn't make *me* up." Her hands dropped once again. She takes a few steps back, but doesn't turn, and her voice is straightforward, disarmingly passionless. She swings her arms around as if pointing to the rest of us. "That's why these people hated it – what you wrote – because it was half-truth, and half-truth is worse than a lie because no one knows what to believe."

"Stories are not to be believed," he says.

"If that's true, you never would have written a word," she says. "You *wanted* to be believed. You wanted nothing but to be believed. That's why you gave your life for your work. Don't try to deceive – it doesn't become you, and it never did."

Just exactly what she wants from him, I thought at that moment, was not so easy to name, but what she knew was that she still didn't have it. "We remember when you came and chose your plot up here, some of us do." She didn't raise her voice. "We remember the tears, too, not for dying, but for your marriage – how it broke just then. We remember all of that. We were here."

He looks up at her, amazed.

"Of that you never wrote a word," she says.

"It's in there," he tells her, "that damned agony – it's in there. You can find it all over in my books."

"But not her –"

"She was my wife –"

"And was I somehow less human?" she says. "And with me – you can undress me, you can have your way with me, the whole world watching."

"Not *me*," he says, and for the first time, there's some anger. "It wasn't me up here," and he points at some place that isn't real.

"Yes, you," she says. "Because you are the one who tells all the world how beautiful I am when I lie back on the grass, my hair like some golden halo all around. You are the one who used me – not him, not my husband."

He slouches back against his own stone. I knew him in life, and it's not often he was this speechless; but he hadn't spoken at all to any of us since he'd come, not until Jennie walked over.

"Listen," he said, "I gave you life. When you were dead and gone, I gave you life." And he pointed at her, some shards of old man of sin still glowing in his soul. Takes a while, but time is immaterial.

"You think maybe you're God," she says.

When he responds, it's not really defensive – that's not it. He really believes what he says. "Listen," he tells her, "who would know who you are anymore – you know? No one would pause a moment at your grave, so long ago it was you died. No one would know you."

"You know my name," she says. His face seems gray and empty. "Say it," she says.

"Say what?" he asks, as if he doesn't know what she means.

"Tell me my name – not the name you gave me. Tell me the name by which I was baptized.

I'm not yours."

She stands there waiting, then steps back as if she has forever. She drops her arms from her chest, unbuttons her coat before him, then puts her hands in the pockets. She looks around, sees no one, but she knows better. She knows very well that some of us are here, listening. But she doesn't care. We may listen. She knows we'll want to know, and we all have our own stories.

"You don't even know, do you?" she says, but there's a gracious, soft smile on her lips. "You remember every detail of how you described it between Garrett and I, up here at this secret place, don't you? You told the world. *You* took me here," and she has to reach for words now, " – and all I'm asking of you is my name," she says again, but not angrily. She's not after revenge – that's not it. And even he knows it; he feels it in the pitch of her words. "To you I was nothing more than a character in your story, that's all. Do you know how that feels?" And then again, "Tell me my name."

It's difficult for him to look into her eyes, which is to say, into her soul, so he pulls a hand up across his face as if something is there to wipe away.

Seconds pass. A minute. Two minutes. Her waiting is relentless.

There are no cars coming up the road to the cemetery. Somewhere far away, a dog barks. He knows he could stand here forever and not remember exactly because her name is no longer in the vault of his memory. He remembers her only as Garret's wife, his cousin's wife, but he's never forgotten how he created her story, where he was sitting, how he walked around the room to get the details right, how hard he had worked, how the next morning he went over and over it again, that lovemaking in this secret place. He had to get it right, had to tell it truly – it was such a story around town.

He looks up to see she's still waiting.

"You don't remember," she says. Her shoulders drop. "Admit it. You don't know me at all." She is turning him in her hands. She can. And there is some pain, I'm sure, a rare commodity here – but we all have memories.

It's hard for him to be here with her. Her will is immense.

He's standing there frozen, face empty, her smile growing seemingly more considerate because she knows she has forever. She feels no need to speak. It wasn't how she'd planned it – what she might say, how they might talk – because she hadn't guessed he wouldn't remember her name, not after what he'd done, how much he'd written. But they have arrived where she wanted to take him, where, she might have said, she needed to, for his sake, and hers, too, maybe. For the first time in her life, she is stronger than he is.

But she wasn't thinking of herself. Credit her this: she's been up here for ninety years, and even though time is immaterial – and maybe because it is – there's grace in this woman's spirit and no more spite.

That's why, just then, in his silence, she steps closer to him. It's that simple.

Nothing is said. She remembers he had given her a life that she might not have had – he wasn't wrong. Occasionally, just occasionally, people drive up to the cemetery, get out of the car, and walk to her grave; and she knows – she understands – that when they stand there and read the words her husband had carved in the stone – "Wife of Garret Van Engen," words shadowy with mildew now – when people stand there, people she doesn't recognize, she understands that they are there because of him, because of what he he'd written.

It is ninety years since she'd died, becoming the mother she never would be, and in that time she'd come to understand that if it weren't for this man, few, if any, would ever pause before the stone the way a few still sometimes do. In those first years, people stopped often, some of them – women – even crying, and her folks full of regret for the way they'd handled everything now that their daughter was gone. For years, her father had come, but that was long behind her, and besides, he was here, too – and all of that humiliation and guilt has long ago come up and out of this ground.

What she'd come to understand was not so much that this man had given her life – only God could do that – but that he'd prolonged it, even if the facts weren't square and what he'd written was so much more than he should have. He had their love right, she told herself. That much he'd had right, after all. It was odd and hurtful to read it. Maybe she was more a part of his secret place than she'd ever been in life itself, a place he'd created.

He looked up at her once again, but still without the name she wanted. "I'm sorry," he says.

"It's been so very long."

"You can't use that one here," she tells him, and she comes even closer to him. Once again, she brings her hands up to his elbows, then pulls herself near him, has him, this big man, in her grasp. "You really don't know, do you?"

He has to force himself to look into her eyes, and he's struck by the fact that there is nothing menacing there. He shakes his head.

"Not even a guess?" she asks.

What he sees in her eyes is something he doesn't remember ever seeing before, something it takes him some time to understand. It's shocking in it guilelessness, and it seems like nothing human he'd ever seen. He remembers, as a boy, being told about it, what it might be – this grace; but it's taken his death for him to see this odd phenomenon for real, if this can be said to be real. And because there seems no anger, he opens himself in a way he hadn't before, this writer who, for so many years, opened himself to his readers. "You're Garret's first wife," he says. "You're Jenny, aren't you?"

She's been holding him at the elbows, but with those words her small arms circle his broad chest and she holds him tenderly as a lover, not a lover in any sense he might remember, either, but a lover that is, as she is, not of this world.

She backs away slightly, lets his arms go for a moment, then reaches for an elbow again and gently pulls him with her. "And there's others here, too," she says. "I'm not alone after all. This is a good place."

For the first time, he smiles. "I know *where* you are. I remember your stone – when it was new. I used to come here. As a boy, I used to come here."

She takes his hand, and the two of them walk back from the fence line.

"There are more," she tells him. "I'm not alone, you know." She gestures with her arm at the cloud of witnesses. "Lots of ghosts around here," she says, making a joke. She is, after all, still something of a girl.

"Others?" he says.

"Lots of them will have something to say, too," she tells him. "You have some explaining to do to these people, writing about them the way you did." She squeezes his arm. "But there will be time."

"I had no idea," he says. "It seemed right to be here, where I was born and reared. When I was a boy, I looked over these fields and wanted to tell their stories."

"It was a good decision," she tells him. Her smile is gracious, as you might expect from someone up here, forgiving.

"Have you thought of your mother?" she asks him.

"She's here?" he says to her.

"You were thinking, somewhere else?" she says.

He knows where her stone stands, of course, so he turns.

They're arm-in-arm now, but as if by instinct, in fear, he takes her hand. "I haven't seen her," he says.

"That doesn't mean she's not here," she tells him. "We're not yours, you know. You thought so for a long time, but we have our own lives, so to speak."

"She could have come by?" he asks. "Like you have – she could have come?" He looks back to his own stone and turns around; the neighborhood isn't all that large.

"You forget that most of us here had minor roles. I was dead in what – fifty pages?" She wraps her hand around his. "Your mother is there in everything you wrote," she tells him. "What's more, she *is* your mother."

"I was just a kid when she died," he says.

"We all know that," she tells him.

The two of them are standing on bare ground beside a tall pine that's rustling in a soft wind, unusually warm for January, a wind reaching up from the south, creating the only sound around them.

"You'll find us more forgiving than we were," she tells him. "Your mother, too, although I don't have to tell you that she always was a saint."

He nods. "Can I speak to her?"

"There will be more now who want to talk to you – we are a community, and always were," she tells him.

"I'll have to wait?" he asks, and she nods.

"Waiting isn't a horror anymore," she tells him, this young thing.

Together, they walk right into the center of things; and when they do, we make a path for them, even though he doesn't see us, and neither does she.

But she knows, so she pulls her hand away from his for a moment and then pushes her arm into his, and he takes it as a gentleman would. The way she walks with him now, arm-in-arm, seems almost bride-like, if you can imagine it, all of us standing there between the stones, admiring.

They are lovers in a sense he never dreamed, the two of them standing together in the cemetery above the town in a fine and secret place, if not an Eden, amid a gathering of shadows, a hundred of them, maybe more, emerging from the moonlit stones all around.

Where the Tree Falls

It was, in a way, like a road trip. Lawrence wanted us along, he told us. That was all he said – he just wanted us with, and then a smile in typical Lawrence fashion. Almost wordless.

No one commands anyone to do anything up here, of course, but then, in glory, nothing we do is tedious. He simply told us one day, as if out of nowhere, how he thought it might be good for our souls to make a visit with him, and there would be a deliverance, some friend of his daughter-in-law somewhere out on the reservation.

His daughter-in-law is not a young woman. For the record, Lawrence himself is a decorated World War I vet, so his son (had he lived) and his wife (not his first) are, in your world, old people. But Magenta, a lovely name, I thought, wasn't the person dying. He knew the soul being delivered only because the man was a grandson of someone he'd known as a boy, when he still lived out in South Dakota.

By the way, Lawrence is mostly here, with his wife. Once in a while, he and Gertie take a leave and spend some time out west.

It was something of an unusual request because Lawrence really doesn't want much, so we went with.

The braids in Magenta's steel-gray hair made obvious she was full-blooded, although Lawrence told us that her father was actually Cheyenne. Up on the porch of her four-room house on the windswept prairie, the screen on her front door needed replacing, Bill Versluis said – and he was right – but don't think him judgmental. Billy spent most of his retirement employed by women who needed help with their leaky faucets and stubborn storm windows. The faded toys left scattered all over her front yard meant there were frequent visits by grandchildren or great-grandchildren.

I'm trying to be careful here, but let me just say it this way – it wasn't a place you'd find in Highland, very small and somewhat memorably untidy. But these days, every last one of us is aware that messes have nothing to do with salvation, something of a hard lesson for Dutch Calvinist people to get straight. The truth is, we found the place inviting. You think that's just spin, but it's not. It's pure joy not to make judgments. You'll love it, I swear.

The strange thing about Magenta Where the Tree Falls is that she seemed to know that we were there, just a circle of old friends who'd come in respectful silence for a cup of coffee from the percolator jumping around on her stove. She's a large woman with a broad and happy face, crossed by a dozen lines as deep as the tracks a thundershower leaves in a field just-plowed.

She'd pulled some kind of sweet bread out of the stove, just before we arrived, and the smell was divine – trust me on that. We stood there in her kitchen, a couple of us took chairs, and we watched her work, gently taking that bread out of the pan, then wrapping it in tin foil, *used* tin foil, from the back of her silverware drawer, then putting that loaf down beside an old honey bucket half-full of chicken soup she'd already covered. The whole time she was at it, I felt as if one of us was holding a camera because she worked in such a way as to not block our view. Strange, her being so considerate. A delight.

She put it all in a Styrofoam bucket with a wire handle, and left it there on the kitchen table while she prettied herself in a bathroom so small we couldn't have peeked if we'd tried. That's overstatement, of course, but we were on Lawrence's turf just then so we looked to him for what was and wasn't proper, and he sat there at the table, his long legs crossed, his wife, Gertie, beside him, both of them waiting politely. We were somehow going with.

There were no new appliances in that kitchen, and the furniture was bargain-basement, at best; otherwise, the place looked a good deal like it might have been an apartment in your ordinary old-folks home – that old white man praying over a loaf of bread up on the wall, a church calendar with smiling African kids by the light switch, and a tumult of school pictures stuck to the refrigerator door, all of them just a bit more dark-skinned than you'd ever see in Highland.

Magenta was going to visit the man who was dying. It wasn't her deliverance we were there for, it was someone else, Lawrence had told us.

When the doorbell rang, we all jumped. We weren't expecting company.

It was Lucas, her great-grandson. Magenta pulled him into her ample bosom when she let him in, and I looked at Lawrence again, wondering whether he just wanted us to see this progeny of his way over here in South Dakota. Meanwhile, I couldn't help but wonder if this was the way things were done on the reservation – grandmas taking grandkids to a deliverance as if it were some kind of community gathering.

Lawrence smiled. He had his hand on his wife's.

"You think he'll like it?" Lucas said when he spotted the Styrofoam pail. "What'cha got in there, Grandma?"

She told him, and he nearly swooned in a kid-like way, so she grabbed another loaf of that sweet bread she'd wrapped in tin foil and stowed in the cupboard, opened it, and cut off a healthy slice, spread it with butter from the butter bell, put it on a plate, and laid it down before his hungry eyes right there at the table. Lawrence and Gertie were all goofy – this Lucas was theirs, too, after all, a couple of grands back or so. Makes little difference. They're all yours, finally.

"Mr. Lovell going to die, Grandma?" the little boy asked her.

"Seems that he is, Lucas," she told him, "much as anyone knows those things." "Rainy says it's not fair," he said. "She says he was the best teacher she ever had."

"Don't suppose anything's fair," Magenta told her grandson. "Don't suppose none of us can count on things ever really being fair in this world." She was buttoning a sweater, but she stopped to lay a hand on his shoulder. "I'd take his place, Lucas," she said, "if it were my time and I could just sit in for him."

The boy stopped mid-bite and looked at her as if he had to concentrate to imagine her gone. "When do you think you're going to die?" he asked her. "You're already really old." "Don't I know," she said. "Time'll come, of course. Now you go on and finish that apple bread, and then we better get going or maybe Donell will pass along before we get there." That's how it went, almost eighty years between the two of them. I was already glad we'd made the trip, and we hadn't even come to the bedside of the man – a young teacher, I guess – who was dying.

Just a word about Lawrence. After all, there aren't many Yankton Sioux in Highland Cemetery. He beams when he says it, but he can't help bring it up whenever someone new comes around and looks at him strangely. What he says in his quiet way is that no one in town, not a soul, could have ever guessed – or would have – that someday he and his wife, Geertje, nee de Groot, hard-headed Milford de Groot's own daughter, would someday celebrate their fiftieth wedding anniversary; but they did, 1972, very successfully, in the big church in the middle of town, just a half-mile north of the spot in Vander Aa's cornfield where he'd quite tenderly gotten Jennie pregnant.

She was 17 back then. He was 23. She was still at home, taking care of her brothers and sisters, all nine of them. Lawrence was a vet and a hero and a full-blood Yankton Sioux with an Indian name he hadn't used since he started school out east, "Where the Tree Falls."

Gertie's getting pregnant was one of those things, people say, that just about everybody knew, but nobody talked about in public. There may have been a time when a gang of locals might have got together vigilante-style and made sure that Lawrence the Indian never, ever got another white girl pregnant. But at the time, even the bigots would have said that Lawrence wasn't your ordinary redskin.

Still, Milford threw his daughter out and threatened the life of the Indian. But Highland isn't Dodge City, and wasn't back then, either. Besides, Lawrence Where the Tree Falls was congressionally-decorated, a man who came to work on the De Bey farm after carrying son George out of a muddy trench in France, bullets blazing all around, a gesture for which George and his father swore they'd be forever grateful.

To say Lawrence and George were buddies over there in France would be pushing things, but son George's eyes were wide open when Lawrence slung him over his shoulder – he's a big guy – and carried him back to a spot beyond grenades.

George took a bullet back, but once the Army surgeon cut it out of the muscle of his right leg and handed it to him, he carried it in a box like a diamond ring and never forgot the way Lawrence, a square-shouldered pack mule, determined to save the white doughboy's life. He promised Lawrence anything once they both got out, and Lawrence took him up on the offer.

Now you might think that strange – I mean that Dakota Lawrence didn't go back to the reservation; but "How Ya Gonna Keep 'Em Down on the Farm after They've Seen Paree?" didn't play only in the heads of white boys. What's more, when Lawrence enlisted, he did so in Pennsylvania, where he'd been going to school, a thousand miles and more away from the Yankton Reservation he'd once called home. He'd been there for just about ten years, even spent his summers with white folks in a variety of places out east. So when he came home to the reservation, the reservation didn't seem like home. There were no bathtubs, no work to speak of, and lots of alcohol – lots and lots of it.

What we all know now is that Lawrence wasn't exactly in love with Geertje de Groot when he started diddling her, and – let me try to say this kindly – Geertje never actively opposed his diddling. But the two of them, not so much unlike each other as you might think, never left each other's side after what they thought they consummated amid the tasseled August corn in that eighty that Vander Aa farmed, not all that far from town.

Meanwhile, Milford, her father, fiery and proud and way over-religious, spit and sputtered and swore about this new country he'd come to not all that long ago, swore to high heaven that were he still in his beloved Holland, there'd be hell to pay for what that Indian had done to his oldest daughter, when most of town understood clearly that Geertje wanted nothing more than to get out of his house of horrors. He called in the church to do his dirty work, but the De Beys weren't without their own power – and they knew Gertie too. He left, took his wife and five his children – two wanted to stay – and returned to his blessed Holland, was never heard from again.

Geertje confessed her sin to the church – those things happened back then – married Lawrence and, contrary to most people's predictions, fell in love, and him with her too.

Lawrence and Gertie are both at rest here in the Highland Cemetery, of course, as is one of their daughters, who died of ovarian cancer. A second daughter lives on a bluff above the Mississippi, just across the river from LaCrosse, Wisconsin. Two sons farm the place Lawrence did, and then some. Another is a doctor in Santee, Nebraska, the other a retired teacher in Sioux Falls. They're all dark-skinned, if you're wondering. They all have their father's hair, but two of them have their mother's blue eyes, quite beautiful people, if you're wondering.

One child, the last one, a boy named Richard, got it in his head to live the way Lawrence's parents had, so he moved back to the reservation his father left, got himself an Indian wife, Magenta, who's really half Cheyenne, and stayed there. His hair was long and braided and almost perfectly silver when he died and left Magenta alone, and he and his wife went by the name of "Where the Tree Falls." For most of his life he dabbled in the tribe's bison herd, becoming something of an expert. You might have seen him on TV once in a while. Even got in a couple of advertisements – he was that good looking. Cameras loved Richard de Groot Where the Tree Falls.

But this story is about Lawrence's daughter-in-law, Magenta Where the Tree Falls, a woman, an elder.

So, anyway, we piled into the back of the pickup when Magenta and Lucas left down the road. Great fun, and a long ride, since she was bound for what used to be a town, a port, in fact, a place named Greenwood, all the way down to the Missouri River, most of the way across the reservation. Lewis and Clark stopped there years ago, and a baby they held in their arms, a man called Struck by the Ree, was sitting elegantly on a bluff just above town when we passed. Lawrence waved respectfully, as did we. As did he.

"He made sure the white man didn't get the pipestone," Lawrence told us. "You know? – the monument." He nodded roughly north as if Minnesota were just across the section. "Some hated him for putting his mark on the treaty, but he made sure we would always have the red stone for our pipes."

"You don't even smoke, Lawrence," Bill Versluis said, "at least I never saw you with a Camel."

He laughed. "A pipe is not a Camel."

Some of us are faster than others, but now that we're gone, we all pick up cues far more quickly than any of us ever did.

Coming down that hill, I realized I hadn't spent enough time along the Missouri Valley during my lifetime. The hills roll as triumphant as billowing clouds, sandstone cliffs here and there like tawny whitecaps on an ocean of hills on both sides of a wily river that, years ago, spread out in some places almost ten miles wide. Honestly, I told myself, I could guess why a man like Lawrence wasn't known for talking – there was simply nothing to say in a landscape as near to being eternal as where we were just then, coming slowly down to the river.

"How come people have to die?" Lucas asked his grandma. We were in the back of the pickup most of the time, but never out of earshot.

"Dying is something all of us do, almost like breathing," she told him. "We start to breathe the moment we're born, and then sometime we stop and that is what we know of this life."

"Donell Garland is not old like you," Lucas said. "How come he's going to stop?"

"You honeybear," she said, turning to him a moment, wrapping her hand around the back of his neck. "Some questions take whole lifetimes to answer – and then some." She turned back to the road's gentle curls. "Look there," she said, and she pointed at the tribe's buffalo herd, who happened to be grazing right across the road from the grave of Struck by the Ree, a stone's throw from the river. "The buffalo are here, too."

The boy twisted around a bit to watch. They were very close to the road. "Will the buffalo be at your house, too, Grandma?" Lucas said.

Everyone knew what the little boy meant, and like Lucas, we waited for an answer.

"Yes, of course they will be there when I go," she said, and she pulled him beside her into a hug as we pulled up at the stop sign at the bottom of the hill. "And yours, too."

All of us – we liked that.

Two children played on plastic trikes just outside the door to Donell's trailer, his children, we figured. The two of them called Magenta "Grandma" when she came up, even though by blood she wasn't. It was their father, Donell, who was dying, and that he had little time to live appeared obvious when we saw him in the bed just off the living room, gaunt and skeletal, his throat already full of the phlegm that creates that telling cough.

Two women stood in the kitchen drying dishes, one of them his wife, we figured, the other maybe her mother, or his. They were speaking softly when Magenta knocked, then put her arm around Lucas's shoulder as if to make clear to them that the boy was here to learn from what he saw, and not just stay out front with the kids.

No one spoke. All smiled. Magenta and Lucas took three steps up and in, and Lucas gave the young woman the sweet bread. She smiled, whispered her thanks, kissed Magenta on the cheek, and returned the hug Magenta had initiated, the two of them holding each other for a few endearing seconds. The woman – her name was Iris – pointed to the bedroom.

I was saying that we pick up cues rather quickly these days, or at least no one stays in the dark for very long. Right then, for the first time, I realized this wasn't just a tourist thing, nor was it the kind of visit where the locals needed a hand, nor was it a showcase for Lucas, that beautiful great-great grandson. Lawrence Where the Tree Falls Gibson wasn't taking us along home to relieve our boredom, either. Magenta had Lucas with, just like Lawrence had us along, because there were things we had to see to learn, "good for the soul," he'd said. Hard as it may be for you to understand, dying doesn't mean there's nothing left to learn – learning is just more of a blessing.

Lucas sat on one side of Donell Garland, and Grandma on the other. For some time, neither of them said anything at all. Donell's eyes were closed, once in a while, a flutter, which couldn't have been enough for him to recognize his visitors.

"Could anyone just come in here and see him?" I asked Lawrence.

Lawrence shook his head, meaning Magenta, for some reason, was special.

A torn quilt was thrown over his gaunt body. Donell was so thin his bones looked peaked even under the covers, his face sallow and worn – he seemed fifty years old, although those children suggested he was much younger, as did his wife. It was cancer, lung cancer, even though he'd never smoked. That he was in the last throes was evident.

When the two of them spoke finally, it was a one-sided conversation, mostly not about anything at all. Donell muttered things to her that had little or no meaning, all of it delivered in a plaintive tone she would thank him for over and over, then bless him with her hands, place them on his face, on his arms and shoulders, thank him as if she understood perfectly everything he said or intended.

Mostly it was quiet and silent. His wife came by, and his mother-in-law. There were sufficient seats for all three of them surrounding the bed, but no one spoke, not the boy, either. It was as if silence itself was a distinguished gentleman come to pay respects and pray in peace. None of us spoke, either, all of us watching Lawrence, because this scene was as altogether reverent as Lawrence simply assumed it would be.

Soon enough, strangely, I swear, I felt something I'd never quite felt before at any deliverance, a palpable sense of the imminence of death, as if it were something not so much to be hated, but, in a way, honored, by all of us, the living and the dead, even the boy Lucas, sitting in perfect silence in a bedroom not much larger than the bed of that old pickup in which we'd driven up in. And it was there with us, death itself, a presence.

Then Magenta whispered something about the soup and lifted the top off the honey bucket, produced a spoon from her apron, and ladled a taste up to his lips. She took a clean hand towel from another pocket, tucked it under his chin, and lifted the back of his head to prop a pillow beneath.

Plainly, it was too much, so she took a chunk of bread from her apron pocket, unwrapped it from the cellophane and dipped it into the broth. Somehow he found that small bit of dipped bread easier. Magenta helped him.

Almost miraculously, we thought, he thanked her in the Dakota language. It was a transaction I'd never seen before, and I understood it only because I am these days who I am. Magenta's eyes went moist, filled with tears she carefully kept from spilling, but couldn't really hide, either from us or from the living. And I knew somehow that Donell had graced Magenta at that moment, had respected her, and thereby loved her for what she'd offered and given him. There was honor in that room at that moment, something you don't always see and never in exactly the way we just had, death and honor.

I looked at Lawrence, but he wasn't thinking about me or what I was seeing. Gertie was the one who lent me the knowing smile. She understood, because she knew I did. Donell was dying, but giving Magenta the kind of respect that helped her understand he would be without a doubt in loving hands after his breath was gone. That was the transaction. Amazing.

She leaned over and whispered something only the dead could hear, and she said it in the Dakota language. No matter, of course. "Have you seen your relatives?" she asked him, although those words seem flat in English. Maybe "Have you seen all of those who love you?" – something like that.

Donell's eyes opened slightly and he offered enough of a nod to help us all see that it was an assent. Yes, he told her, he'd seen those he loved.

I looked, once again, across the bed at Gertie, who, as politely as she could, pointed directly behind me at a gathering that had assembled, it seemed, out of nowhere, a gallery of Yanktons and Cheyenne in buckskin and blankets, beaded and blessed. There they were, behind and around us, like a raiding party, a host of them arranged in a semi-circle. I never felt quite so much like a paleface, and I've got lots of practice in being invisible.

It was Donell who held the eyes and the attention of the folks behind us, but also Magenta, who likely would be joining them soon, and even the boy, Lucas, who like all children, lights up the eyes of the old, the infirm, and all of those already gone.

When I turned back to Gertie, she wasn't looking at me or thinking of me because suddenly, her own dead son had come over beside her and her husband, Lawrence, and I couldn't help but thank the Lord for bringing us here, if for no other reason than to witness that sweet reunion. It wasn't the first time they'd been together, but Richard was – or is – their own, their boy, and homecoming is always homecoming, maybe more so when there's a deliverance.

Right there in the middle of all those people, and curtained in this profound silence, Magenta got down on her knees and prayed with Donell, prayed for him, in words that she didn't speak aloud, Lucas listening, eyes closed. We know what she prayed; but sometimes we can say too much and thereby stand in the very way of beauty, like a cloud against the sun, so I'll allow you to imagine what you might say to and about someone dying if he or she was already amid a congregation of witnesses able and willing to admit him to this life, which isn't death. Picture her there yourself, amid the throng, in silence. Honestly, I don't think you'll be far off.

When she got to her feet, she hugged Donell once more, then his wife, then his mother-in-law, then stood at the bedside, Donell having fallen into sleep. She raised her arms to the rest of us, as if to lead us in song. She wore a smile big as the valley around us, wide as the river. She was thanking us, all of us.

Not until we got back did I even wonder about whether or not she actually saw us there in that tiny bedroom packed with ghosts. She was praising God. That's what she was doing. I knew it – we all did. She was giving thanks.

Lawrence made it clear that we should get back in the bed of the pickup when we left. He wanted us to hear how Magenta talked to Lucas, because he knew the boy would be thinking about what he'd seen and what he hadn't.

We jumped in, literally. Magenta pulled out of the driveway, turned down the road along the river, and took a left just outside the village on her way up the hill. But instead of going on, she turned left again into a graveyard where someone had already dug a site for Donell Garland.

She got out slowly – she didn't move fast – and walked over to the grave, Lucas right beside her. A dozen boards lay over the open hole in the ground. "It looks like rain," Magenta said, kicking the boards closer together.

"How come you want to check the grave?" Lucas asked.

She told him rain in the open grave meant someone close to the deceased was going to die, too. She didn't want that. And the boy, I swear, was pondering all these things in his heart.

All told, it was, in a way, one of those guided travel tours a person takes to see what you've never seen, to experience something you knew nothing of, the whole thing directed by Lawrence Where the Tree Falls, but produced by the Almighty himself.

But then, quite frankly, the most astonishing thing of all transpired. The Greenwood Cemetery sits in weeds and stubble just up the blacktop from the corner of the old river road, on the way to Marty, South Dakota. There we sat – Bill, Lawrence and Gertie, Lammie de Lange, Les Meerfeld, and me – in the back of the pickup. If we'd had some gentle mutt along, we'd have been a postcard, reupholstered sons and daughters of the reservation, our old bones renewed enough to take the bumps.

Lawrence stepped out just then, a couple hundred yards up the road. We'd been following his lead since time began that day, so the rest of us hopped out, too, and marched with him up the hill to an obelisk we simply assumed marked the grave of the old war horse Struck by the Ree. We were wrong – it commemorates a treaty, and includes a short list of those who signed, and at the top of list, the name of the old chief, a man christened, in a way, right there at that spot by Lewis and Clark, way back in 1803.

And there he sat, the old man, in leather and leggings, an ornamental shield right beside him, his vest festooned with beadwork and a gadzillion porcupine quills. We'd seen him coming down the river, to Donell's trailer, in fact. He was no surprise.

But right there beside him was a chrome-domed old man with wispy chunks of hair growing out of his ears so profusely that his shiny pate seemed surrounded by clouds. I didn't know him, had never met him. Didn't have a clue.

Gertie walked up to him, Lawrence staying back with the rest of us. When she stood there in front of him, the bald man got up from the ground where he'd been sitting with the chief of the Yanktons. Smoke still rose reverently from a pipe in the chief's hand, a pipe shaped unmistakably from red pipestone.

"Is mother here, too?" she asked, somewhat awkwardly. He nodded.

She looked back at Lawrence, who for the first time since we'd crossed the state line, seemed surprised.

"And you were there, too? – in the trailer with Donell?" she asked the man that had to be her father.

He nodded, a short man, squat, like the famous Yankton who now stood beside him. Lawrence is twice as tall, his own daughter a half foot taller at least. But Milford de Groot held out both hands, a smile across his face as serene as anything I've seen in the beyond; and she took his hands herself, slowly, guardedly, almost humanly in fact, before finally walking into his arms.

In your terms, it was all of seventy-five years since they'd seen each other – more, of course, since they'd held each other, if that had ever happened at all since Gertie was toddler. Old Milford was hardcore, after all, a staunch old Dutchman who thought tone of voice was more than enough to express love, even to family, even to children. His thick arms came up around his oldest daughter.

And just at that moment, I swear, down the hill and over the cemetery we'd just left, the crowd that had assembled for the internment was slowly walking away from the grave, when up behind them, on clouds that billowed up the way they can on summer afternoons, a band of Yanktons and Cheyennes walked their ponies up against the sky. I saw them.

Lucas was stunned, and so was I. There we all stood, all of us, beside a granite obelisk set right there to commemorate a treaty of peace 150 years ago, and Lawrence Where the Tree Falls with his arm up over the stocky shoulder of his father-in-law.

Just across the road, as promised, the tribe's own herd of buffalo held their huge heads up in the breeze as if to catch the scent of something delightful, even endearing.

And Magenta told Lucas – "These are things you should never forget."

That's what she said right then on the hill above the Missouri.

Deliverance

When it comes to seeing and knowing, we've got a leg up on most of you. But then, only The Maker has total omniscience, so now and then we suffer false alarms – *we* meaning squads of old friends or fishing buddies beckoned for what we call "a deliverance." Things don't always go according to plan.

Old-timers say deathbed ritual was a bigger deal one hundred years ago, when small crowds formed around those on their way up the hill, family and friends gathering to hear some parting blessing or the final utterances of a man or a woman bound for glory, as if whatever the dying might divulge were something akin to gospel. Such gatherings weren't as silly as they might sound – take it from someone who's been there, both on the bed as well as hanging around, spook-like, waiting for someone like Tom Holland, the postman, to go. Old Tom was the man who, up until my own death, had quite regularly stopped for coffee when he delivered the mail. "Ten minutes," he'd say pointing two fingers, scrupulously. Often enough it was twenty, but the mail always got through.

When he died, I was there. Attending a deliverance is good work, among the finest you can draw up here. Mostly. People are serious at that moment, deadly serious. Sorry.

You might think that what's said at a man or woman's death bed could prompt a snicker from us, given what we know and they don't; but we're bigger than that. Besides, all of us remember when we, too, saw through a glass darkly – which doesn't imply that we're clairvoyant, either.

Mailman Tom just wore out. That happens. He'd never married, had no kids, but wasn't lacking for friends, me among them. My office wasn't the only stop on his route. He knew everyone, went to every ball game the high school ever played, and almost always wore a winning smile one simply doesn't see all that often down in the vale of tears. Let me put it this way – and take it from a veteran – Old Tom Holland didn't change much when he got up here. I'm serious. In life already, Tom was something of an angel.

Okay, that's stretching it.

He died at home, as he wanted. And we were there, four or five of us, taking up no space. Among the living were Wilma, his only sister, and Wilma's two girls, MaryAnn and Betts – and a baby. You don't regularly find a baby at a deathbed, but MaryAnn couldn't get a sitter for her little one, not so much a tail-ender as the last in an almost endless string. And it was a joy for us to have that child there since we don't often share a room with a toddler. You're never too old or dead, for that matter, to forget what pure joy a child can be. The little girl sat silent as a toad, as if she knew what was in the offing. Tom's preacher was there, of course. It wasn't tight, just comfy.

The Hollands are solid singers, Wilma a choir member since the late Fifties, her daughters-in-law often singing duets in church, so when they broke into "Abide With Me," it was, even for us, quite touching, Wilma holding her brother's hand. We sang along, which gave the music even more girth than they were capable of giving or hearing. After that harmony, we were ready to take him with us up the hill, and they were ready to let him go.

But old Tom didn't play along. It wasn't his time, exactly, so you might call it a false alarm – like I said, we're not all-knowing, either. When he fell off to sleep, we all waited – and waited, and waited; and then the nurse came in and shrugged her shoulders because she didn't know how to call it, and the fact is, no one does, exactly, although there are a dozen or more odd stories about the dying actually predicting their time, to the hour. Not this one. Tom's eyes closed, but his breathing eased, as if he'd decided maybe another dream or two would be just fine for the time being.

Reluctantly, the women and the baby left a half-hour later or so, when the nurse assured them she'd call, should something happen.

Two days later, we all gathered again, and once more the women sang "Abide with Me," plus, this time, "Blessed Assurance," "Trust and Obey," and "Leaning on the Everlasting Arms." All of it, in waiting. This time there was no baby.

"You can go now," Wilma told her brother, hand-in-hand with him. "You don't need to stay."

People say tender things like that, which is why a deliverance is a good assignment. Most often, you get to see people at their best, a blessing all its own.

Tom's eyes wandered around the room – they wore that pallor between gray and blue – and then he said, "They're here for me. I see 'em."

He was talking about us.

That happens. People get close and they see visions.

MaryAnn looked around, straight at us, in fact, blind as a boxcar. "Maybe there's angels hovering," she told her daughters, a description that felt quite honorable, but clichéd.

"My time is up, I think," old Tom said. His false teeth were out, so not everything came out all that clearly, but we could catch his drift. And then he managed a smile. "I'll just be up the road, anyway," he told his sister and his nieces. "I can see now," he said, "and it's not all that far away. They're here all right."

No need to shush him. What Tom told his sister is not something people normally utter on their death beds, so we found it a little revealing, as if the four of us were suddenly in our underwear right there in front of the ladies.

"*Who's* here, Uncle Tom?" MaryAnn said. She's a straight-haired girl who, we all know, has taken a lot during her short life.

"Snooker," he said, slowly. He wasn't all that wrong – Jed and Cal and I were regulars at the table at the senior center a decade or so ago.

No matter. The three women looked pleasingly at each other, smiles that have been all too rare in their lives.

Tom's eyes blinked hard and quick, as if something got caught up beneath the lids. And then he steadied himself into the Doxology, perfectly fitting and in character. But there wasn't much oomph, nor much tune left in him, nor enunciation, so we were the only ones who picked up that old favorite.

"It's up the hill," he told those women. "It's just up the hill where I'm going to."

"I think he's talking about the cemetery," Wilma said. "I bet he's talking about the graveyard."

"Not heaven?" MaryAnn said, as if hurt somehow.

"He must be talking about the cemetery," Wilma told her. "I don't know what's going on in his head. Who knows?"

I think it's better they don't know. Besides, who am I to question The Maker?

"Finally," Tom said, but that's all. Then again, "Finally."

And then, as if he knew the curtains were coming down, he opened his eyes, looked at his loving sister and her two daughters, and whispered, "It's snowing, isn't it?"

It was the mid-June, and no one was thinking snow but Tom. So what? – not everything makes sense. Who knows why he got a kick out of the snow so suddenly? Up the hill, after some snowy nights, everything sparkles, a newborn quilt shivering with diamonds in the swelling moonlight. Maybe he saw the pearly gates like a first pure snow.

And then he went. Or came. That was it, the moment. He rose out of that deathbed as if he were commanded to do so, and we were there like proper church ushers to lead him home.

Okay, it wasn't as dramatic as some, but all of us thought the whole thing was vintage old Tom. Very sweet. We were ennobled, at least that's what it felt like.

I've never attended a deliverance like that without noting that something happens to those who haven't yet departed, in this case to Wilma and her daughters. They believe they've experienced something profoundly holy, something rich with life, even though it's death.

Tom sat up from that bed and looked straight at us, his charmed face wearing that same wholesome smile. We took his hand to help him up the hill, as is our task, although we stayed, respectfully, for the preacher's prayer, which was aimed at them – at Wilma and her daughters, those left behind, and rightly so because Tom didn't need anyone's prayers just then. They did, as is always the case – and as I now hope to prove.

It was all women at Tom's bedside because Harold, of Wilma, was busy in the field, I think – or busy, anyway, and only a brother-in-law, not a brother. Harold has a thousand acres out west where the land starts to roll up to the comely shoulders of the Big Sioux, and he was more than a little ornery about Uncle Tom having left his considerable fortune to the town (library remodeling), the school (a grade school gym), and some church relief agencies. Oh yeah, and Habitat, for whom Tom had worked for twenty years on weekends and even during vacations. Wilma got none because of her husband Harold, who didn't need it and wanted it more than any human being should. We know all of this, of course. Tom told us.

Tom said he'd told his sister a year ago already that they weren't getting much, once it became clear that his brother-in-law never once wore a smile of the kind Tom was never seen without. Harold was just about everything Tom wasn't, voraciously hungry to build a kingdom – his own. Tom always claimed he didn't hate his brother-in-law, but simply couldn't be in a room with him much longer than it took to throw down a Thanksgiving turkey.

Harold, and a few others, believed Tom Holland was gay because he'd never married and almost certainly could have, Harold being the kind of man who couldn't believe that a real man could live without sex.

Certainly he couldn't. What Harold thought about his brother-in-law's sexual preference may have well been true, but some of us, at least, never stopped to ask.

Meanwhile, you know what they say about death and taxes, and brother Harold hated both of them, although he certainly thought less about death until the Grim Reaper himself rode up to his place, looked him in the eye, and told him that he, Harold Fridsma, was going by way of lung cancer. In a way – and I can say this – cancer was a providential choice for Harold, a slow, lingering demise. It gave him time, and having lived his life, he needed time.

I should also mention that neither of Tom's nephews were there when Tom died because like the old man, they were just plain too busy. And mad. And sometimes even a little ashamed of their Uncle Tom the mailman, whom they jokingly referred to as the "'not-mailman." Once upon a time, most men up here would have called those boys – and their old man – assholes, but no more, even though they were and are. It's just that we don't use that kind of language, at least not often, but I'll let it stand a sentence or two back because it's true, and I'm only saying what would have been widely heard.

There's an old water pump out back of Harold and Wilma's farm place, something Wilma decorates with a basket of flowers in late spring, but pretty much useless otherwise, except if you jump on the handle long enough to bring up a trickle of rusty water. Harold was on his way out back one day, when he tripped on a crack in the sidewalk that he knew was there, but it caught him anyway. He stumbled for three drunken steps and fell, banged his head just above the ear off the iron spout of that old pump, and knocked himself out cold.

Wilma looked out her kitchen window and saw him lying in the grass, no blood to speak of, because the open wound he took from that pump was on the side of his head she couldn't see. She thought him dead – she'd been after him for forty years to stop smoking, but when she got outside she saw the blood and realized it was just a fall.

Again. It had happened before, three times in the last few weeks. Once more, he just hadn't picked up his size-fourteens high enough to clear a sidewalk bump, or a root from dry ground, or something else poking up in the barn or yard. He was falling way too often, and this time, since he needed stiches, she took him off to Doc Carpenter, who told him it was time they did some tests. That's when cancer came riding up with staff and hood. Not really. I'm just being literary.

Now there's a part of this story that I can almost skip over because it's pretty much cliché. Think of Levi, the priest, and his ornery sons. Think of King Lear and his daughters. I'm sometimes not sure of what Jesus said about money being the root of *all* evil – after all, Tom and a dozen others don't have a dime's worth of Silas Marner in them. But some do. Many. Especially out here, where a thousand acres – what with ethanol and corn prices – means you'll need a loader just to cart the loot away when some old landowner takes his place up here with us. We're talking millions, and I'm not kidding. It takes real saintliness not to get bamboozled by that level of pay-off.

And Harold's boys were not saints. Or angels. Everett de Haan told us the bank refused their business a few years ago, when it became clear that the two of them were spending too much time at the new casino out there on the state line.

Nothing nurtures the soul like a date with the hangman, they say, and for Harold Fridsma, cancer became, simultaneously, his destroyer and his redeemer. When finally it killed him, it also gave him life. For the first time, he found himself growing more and more powerless, which just happens to be the prescribed attitude for those who want to know blessings of faith. His cancer cured him, like bacon or wine or a good cheese; so when his time came – his bedside leave-taking – the strife was o'er, the battle done. All of this, we knew.

Once again, we came down the hill, this time for old Tom's brother-in-law, Harold, who once upon a time would have had more than his share of enemies up here, if we didn't quite miraculously shed grudges. Let's just be clear – we all think coming down the hill for deliverance is an honorable task, and we're not above the rejoicing that quite naturally occurs when some wandering sheep is retrieved from "out on the hills away, far off from the gates of gold," as the old hymn goes, even though the line is overwritten.

Let's say this about Harold Fridsma – he is himself a child of his own upbringing, a man who did absolutely everything with a passion, everything connected with his work, that is. He had an eighth-grade education, milked cows already at seven years old, a fact he never let anyone forget. To him, work was fulfilling, *and* redemptive. He *did* church because it was part of the ritual of his life, like the seasons, a discipline that came to mean something to him only in those months when he became more and more powerless. Cancer gave him four years and six months to think, and in that time he became his own hanging judge. All that stuff about the death of the old man – it's not just conventional wisdom. We know. Blessed Harold cried more tears in the last few months than he had in seventy-some years. Credit him that.

And I'll never forget this, either – how, once we got to that hospital room, Tom, his brother-in-law, already one of us, cried, joy flowing from his ample soul, that lovely smile still there.

The doctors offered some creative measures to him to keep him alive, more machines to hook him up to, more hardware, more options; but he chose to go. Maybe we're prejudiced, but up here, those kinds of decisions we tend to applaud.

So for Harold Fridsma that final leave-taking held no real mysteries, no possibility of a false alarm. The doctor was turning off the switch, so we knew we weren't returning empty-handed.

And they were all there, Wilma and her daughters and their husbands, sober-faced and antsy, two men old enough only to be seduced into thinking they're still in their prime.

They're not tattooed and ear-ringed. Dick and LeRoy Fridsma, lean and mean, specialize in all-night hog barbeques and all manner of wheeling and dealing with their considerable wealth. They are not above work, either, not in the least lazy; but they didn't inherit their father's passions and never once saw their work as redemptive. For them, nothing really was, save weekends at the lake cabin their father built, a play-time palace. I feel unkind for saying all of that, but mostly, all we deal with these days is truth, God help us.

Here's the picture. We're at home, in Harold's living room, where his wife moved his bed six months previous. One of those aerial views of the farm hangs on the wall opposite the picture window, but it's badly faded and tells only half the story since the Fridsmas run cattle elsewhere and own such sizeable chunks of Iowa land that, should some aerial photographer take a portrait now from several hundred feet higher, Harold's land, marked in red or something, would turn the surrounding sections checkerboard. Above the dining room table an old man prays over a half loaf of bread. Faded, too. The only new pictures in the room are a half-circle of grandchildren on a coffee table at the foot of the bed, where Harold could see them.

Ample chairs – even a couple from the kitchen – and a leather corner couch offer plenty of seating. The women are standing, the boys seated, arms up over the shoulders of the couch, legs crossed, both wearing their Sunday Tony Lamas. No grandchildren, except in pictures.

And Tom the mailman is here, Jake Tuinstra, Cal Soodsma, and myself, the old snooker teams, inconspicuous as always, except to Harold, who seemed to notice us the moment we came in – that's how close he was.

And let's be clear here. What every last human being in that room knew – as did we – is that for forty years or more, while what relationship existed between Harold and Wilma Fridsma might well have been defined as a marriage, it was little more than mutual co-existence, Harold being a man almost beyond love. Wilma was forsworn to the oath she took one cold day in May, convicted beyond doubt that a broken marriage was a summons to hell. That they'd stayed together, locked up as they were, wasn't necessarily odd or unusual around here; but elsewhere, I think, it would have been, to many, something of a horror.

But all that brokenness died with the cancer, once Harold really needed to be loved. And Wilma, too, in her undying faithfulness – and her husband's stark need – began to think of Harold's illness almost as if it were a blessed second chance, the first forty years thankfully dead and gone.

When he spotted us first outside that picture window, looking in, he asked, "Who's going to take care of Wilma?" We don't have much to do with such questions, of course. "I'm ready," he said, "but leaving her is tougher than grizzle. I could just cry." He shook his head. "It's taken me most of my life to understand what a good woman she is. What did I know?" And then he squinted. "You here for me, right?"

We nodded, and walked right through that window to take a place out of the way.

"I'm ready," he told us. All he could move was his eyes, but he firmed up his lips in a way that even those in the room understood as a commitment to get this life over and start in on something he knew very little of, a cadre of ushers ready to show him to his place up the hill. He was ready to die.

"You got anything to say to your father?" Wilma asked just then, smiling to those sons of theirs. Begging, really.

Dickie undid his legs and then swung them the other way, just as he did to that chunk of tobacco in his lip.

"There's so much I did wrong," Harold told us. They didn't hear him. "Shush now," Tom told him. "Plenty of time for that later."

"I'm leaving a train wreck," he said.

"Matter of a few moments and that'll be history," Tom told his brother-in-law.

"Well?" Wilma said to her sons, pointing at their father.

Dickie didn't know where to go with his eyes. He never minded his mother all that much, just like the old man hadn't, but it was hard for him to look at his father, to see him laid up like that, snorting tubes, gizmos galore. He was looking directly into the face of death, the skeleton and skulls, and he wasn't seeing his father. He was seeing death and seeing himself – *memento mori*. In that field of study, we know what we see and what we're doing.

"It won't be long and your father will be leaving us," Wilma said.

Dickie, a man with a ready flood of words, stood strikingly bereft.

"See there," Tom told Harold. "Your boy can hardly hold back the tears." Harold's feature-less face still looked skeptical.

"Come here and hold his hand," Wilma told her son. "He's your father, and he's going now. Talk to him," she said, with some bitterness. "He needs to hear you."

Half-truth maybe. She was the one who needed to hear her son say something good. Dickie put his hands down on the leather couch and pulled his angular self up. "Why'n't you take his hand?"

"He can't feel nothing, anyway," LeRoy said.

"Take his hand," she said again, more demanding than she'd been in the last dozen years, and Dickie did as his mother told him.

"Now speak to him," she told him. "Talk to him for once in your life about something besides cattle and beans."

"Is he with us?" Dickie asked.

"He can hear everything – he knows," she told him.

Harold wasn't saying a thing to anyone – to them or us – but he was focused on what was happening.

"This ain't easy," Dickie said.

"You think it's a party for him?" Wilma said. "He's the one dying."

And she was not wrong. That farm house living room was full of folks attending a deliverance, but leave-taking is something one always does all by one's lonesome.

"Go on," Wilma said again.

"I don't even know what to call you," Dickie told him. "He's your father," she told him.

"Sounds like God," Dickie told her because for almost his entire life he'd called the old man, "the old man." "You brought me up right," Dickie said, standing there as if his bunions were killing him. "Working hard, taking care of cattle. And church, too – and to take care of things, take care of the land." He didn't hold his father's hand as much as put his over them. "You taught me just about everything I know." He looked up at his mother. "You taught me to make sure my family had good things."

"Listen to that," old Tom told his brother-in-law. "You hear that, Harold – you hear what your boy is saying?"

Somehow a couple tears got squeezed out of those blurry eyes. Dickie reached down and pulled out his shirttails to find something to wipe their trails from the old man's cheeks, and when he did, something else gave way in him and he started into crying, not sobbing, but real tears.

I'm not lying when I say the two Fridsma boys are roustabouts. The truth is, on those hunting trips to Montana and those Canadian junkets when they catch a couple hundred walleye, they spend lots of time and money in seedy places most Highland folks don't even know exist. Not all that long ago, Dickie went after a babysitter, who was so scared that she never told a soul what happened when he brought her home and stuck a hundred dollars in the pocket of her blouse. I could go on. We're privy to whole stories, not that all the revelations are joyous, let me say.

"I'm going to be better," Dickie said. "I swear it, Pa, I'm going to be better. I'm changing my life now, starting now."

I didn't know what to think. Wilma swallowed almost audibly, but his wife, Betts, looked – I checked – as if the words her husband sang were a melody from heaven.

"Spare me," his brother LeRoy said from the couch, where he sat all arched up like a snake.

"You're such a faggot, Dickie."

Right then, I wished we could have taken hold of one of Harold's limp hands and pulled him up from those machines to take him home and out of there.

LeRoy never got up off that leather couch. He sat there with his legs crossed. "All he's doing, Ma, is trying to get into your tender mercies," he said. "It's pantomime is what he's up to – i'n't, MaryAnn?" I swear she looked like a stone sculpture right out of The Depression. "It's an act," LeRoy said, "and if you buy it, you're dumb as bare ground. It's all about you now, with the old man gone – or going," LeRoy said. "It's all about wooing you, Ma – you're the one holding the deed. That's what's going on here."

"Hold your tongue," Wilma told him.

"It's the plain truth," LeRoy said. "The old man never gave a crap about this. All he ever give us is the back of his hand if we didn't do as we were told. He never loved us a dime's worth, and now my brother is pissing and moaning as if Pa was some saint, which he's not."

LeRoy's wife Betts cowered right then, and I couldn't help wonder what other horrors she'd already lived through. Standing right beside me, old Tom was fit to be tied, but he knows the rules.

"Dickie's got one thing on his mind, and we all know it," LeRoy said, still sitting. "It's just another form of sweet talk, and if you believe him, Ma, then you're even dumber than he is."

"Your father's dying," Wilma said.

"I know," LeRoy said, "but Dickie's not, and neither am I."

LeRoy sat there with his arms crossed over his chest, as if he'd just now finished a hot day's work. Sometimes up here, you forget how cold real live people can be.

"He hears you," Wilma told him. "He hears every word you're saying."

"Well, that'd be a first," LeRoy said. "High time, but don't you think it's a little late?" "Look what he gave you – look at the blessings," Wilma said. "You got more land than anybody in the township – what you think he was working for all those years?" "Me?" LeRoy said. "You think he ever cared a bit about us?"

"Why else would he work as hard as he did? – tell me that."

We couldn't step in and bring some peace. Bedraggled Betts was stiff and lifeless, and Harold himself hadn't said much, except to us. The way I saw it right then, the only people who had a voice in all this dysfunction were the two brothers, their distraught mother, and maybe MaryAnn, Dickie's wife, who was praising the Lord for what He'd just now done in the life of her husband.

"You're the problem here, Ma," LeRoy said, and he finally got up off the couch so that he could stand there a foot taller than his mother, stand there over her like a looming shadow. "My old man goes out of his head when he's dying and gives you control of everything, like an idiot – I mean, what do you know about the damn business?"

Wilma had a look on her face that wasn't far afield of what you see when clouds come up like huge fists of storm.

"And now I got to go through you all the time when I think there's things we can do to build up what we've got? You never had a thing to do with the operation." LeRoy stayed maybe two feet away from his mother, but hovered like a demon. "You're like talking to a kitchen sink."

"Don't go," old Tom said right then to his brother-in-law. "I know you want to, but it's not quite time yet." Harold's creamy eyes looked supplicant and ready. "You still got things to do." Old Tom came up close to a brother-in-law who never had the time of day for him, stood there on the other side of the bed, just beside MaryAnn, who looked like Lot's wife when she once turned her head.

"Get me out of here," Harold said to us.

"Heaven's ready," Tom said, "but you aren't."

"Then coach me through this," Harold said to his brother-in-law, begging.

"Don't talk to me like that," Wilma said to her savage boy. "Don't you talk to your mother like that, LeRoy."

"*He* did," LeRoy said, pointing at the old man, and the truth is, too often in life, he had.

"I'm sorry," Harold said, but we were the only ones who could hear him.

"You're going to want to turn up the volume," old Tom told him. "This family of yours are being a little hard of hearing."

"It don't matter what he said, Ma," LeRoy said. "It don't matter at all because when push comes to shove, I'm taking over. I'm the oldest boy, and that's the way it's supposed to be." He pointed down at his father. "The old man's been gone too long already. His word is suspect – any court'll tell you that."

"Tell him no," old Tom told Harold. "Tell the boy he's way off base. Tell him off, Harold," he said.

Harold tried to shift, but had trouble finding the right gear. He was seeing us better, I think, than he was seeing his family. For months, he'd been thinking about dying, not living, because he knew where he was going. He'd been planning the trip. He was just enough human to know that what he was leaving behind was more trouble than he cared to face.

"I'm the one making the decisions," Wilma told her son, but those words had nothing behind them, and I knew it, and so did Cal and Jake and Dickie and Betts and LeRoy the jackass. Pardon my French.

That's when LeRoy finally came right up in her face, like the bull he is, and said, "Over my dead body. You won't decide anything 'cept when to do dishes."

"Now," old Tom said, and then whispered in his ear.

Somehow God gave Harold the strength and temerity to sit up in that bed, put an elbow behind him, and say, "Don't you talk to her that way." Wasn't garbled, either. Wasn't exactly threatening, but it seemed out of nowhere, out of death itself, and for a moment Harold-come- back-to-life stopped LeRoy dead in his tracks. And then this, more faintly, but just as distinct: "I'm sorry."

It took nearly every ounce of what Harold had left in him for him to lean up that way on his elbow and deliver those few words, but there was enough in him; and all of us – not just old Tom, but all of us – nodded at him as if he were nothing more or less than a prophet.

And there we all stood like an old painting, the grandfather clock tolling, I swear. The dead had spoken; a ghost had come alive.

Then, out of the silence, comes the voice of a woman who hadn't said a thing all afternoon, the voice of MaryAnn the Silent, LeRoy's long-suffering wife, who some would call a saint for putting up with what she has, but most still call a bloody fool.

"You take your land, LeRoy," she told her husband. "You take your land and your tractors and your hogs and your beef and whatever else you're lord over, and you make yourself happy because I'm taking my children and we're leaving."

"You're an idiot," LeRoy said to his wife.

MaryAnn pulled her sweater around her, not as if she were shivering, but as if she was more than ready to take a step outside the cage. "I *am* an idiot," she told him, "but no more."

She walked over to the other side of the bed, took Wilma in her arms, and then turned to her husband and stood there before him, beneath him, really. But from somewhere close to the back forty of that place, she reached back with her right arm and like an ace on the mound wound up and delivered a slap to her husband's face that every soul in that room, dead and alive, saw coming, even though none of us truly believed. "Now go feed your damned hogs," she told him. "Let him die in peace."

No, you shouldn't be thinking, with this whack across the face, MaryAnn Fridsma had actually employed the hand of God. Don't jump to impossibly divine conclusions. LeRoy Fridsma had started and finished more late-night brawls than most of those who live in our valley can count, and he'd taken much tougher blows; but he never suffered one quite so unforeseen.

Still, he walked out of that room in such a way that those boot heels cracked on the hardwood floor, and slammed the door on his dying father as if the war had only begun.

MaryAnn's face didn't change a bit, either. She wore no Uncle Tom smile, her cheeks didn't bloom, and she looked no less bedraggled and beat on than when she'd walked in because she knew the war had only begun. But at least she'd come to understand that there was life after what she'd just now accomplished, something she'd wanted to do for a long, long time.

"Not you, Mom," MaryAnn said. "I'm not leaving you, even if I'm leaving your son." And then she looked down at Harold, who'd fallen off that elbow and was back on the bed, ready to go. "We're going to try – all of us," she said, looking around at Dickie and Betts and Wilma, too. "We're all going to work hard at making this all work," she said. "You go now, Pa," she said. "We're all ready for you to go. Things are going to change."

Harold looked up at old Tom, and Tom held out a hand. It wasn't long, and three of us picked up another resident and brought him with us up the hill.

Deliverance. That was one I won't forget soon.

I turned around while we were on our way up because, you remember, they were singers, all of them, and they went back into "Abide with Me," just as they had with old Tom, and then, once again, there were tears, Harold's cold body right there beside them, husband and father. But this time they had Dickie too, who held a bass line that wasn't bad for a man who hadn't been in church as often as he should have. There's a lot of penitence in that old hymn, but right then, it felt like a fighting song – I swear. Press on.

My wife says to me that sometimes that she thinks it took her eternity before she understood that life really holds no promises for any of us, only deliverance. Sarah's right, of course, when you think about it.

But you can be sure we'll keep an eye out down there. We all will.

It's what we do from up here, mostly. It's what we do, praise the Lord.

Crystal's Visitation

We were reluctant to leave. Well, some of us were.

Well, mostly Crystal, and I can't blame her. She was new, and as I've said before, there's a learning curve. So in sweet and saintly fashion, we stuck around just to be with her because she wanted to stay as long as her earthly remains were there all by their lonesome – I mean, no one anywhere to be seen. I'm serious. There she was, in her casket. But dead. You know.

There'd been some kind of snafu, a mix up between the funeral home people and the family, about time and scheduling, so that somehow, Crystal's mortal coil – nicely displayed, by the way – found itself totally alone against the north wall of the fellowship room at the big church, the mourners gone, the family departed, the funeral director's grief squad dunkin' chocolate chip cookies at the coffee shop downtown. They wear nametags – "So-and-so, Care Assistant." I'm serious. Nobody smiles, either, but then the occasion is a funeral, right? Nobody smiles, anyway.

Oops! – is what I'm saying. I'm not kidding – nothing, or no one, in the fellowship hall but a dead body.

And poor Crystal didn't want to leave it behind, so to speak.

Understandable. I don't blame her, even though our vigil was silly. I mean, who's going to run off with a corpse? And besides, a gang of dead people are going to stop some demented creep? What are we going to do? – scare him to death?

Wait a minute. There's a story.

But it's not this one. This one starts with Crystal's corpse lying in state, alone and abandoned, the church something of a morgue. Bad joke. She's looking quite royal, her husband having gone all out on the coffin, but then he's loaded.

Everyone had departed, including her husband, her second *and* the first, who'd stopped by perfunctorily. That's a judgment, I know, and we're supposed to be above judgments, but we were there and we all saw it, all of us, the living and the dead. The visitation had properly concluded, the family was at Byerly's Eatery, back room, for family-style spaghetti, a special on Wednesday, all you can eat. No one in church, save us and a bag of bones.

I'm being unkind, at least my sense of humor is not coming off as divine. I'll try to clean up my act.

Let me start over. We'd gone down the hill because Crystal Wesselink wanted to visit her own visitation. Is that normal? Well, let's say it's not unusual. Some of us get off the death bed, and even before standing we stamp the blasted dust off our hospital socks. Some of us disappear to destinations unknown, just lift off into hyperspace and are never heard from again. Not all who die end up in the Highland Cemetery. I've said it before – this is not the county jail. Not a soul here is under lock and key.

Most of those who linger wouldn't leave Siouxland if they'd just won the lottery. They wouldn't leave because they grew up on century farms they never left, or because everyone they love is up here on the hill with us. Those who suffer through long and agonizing deaths often accrue more friends and prayer warriors than they would have ever known had they not rolled the truck and died slowly, you know? They stay, too, and most of them drop in on their own visitations.

Me? I didn't, and wouldn't have gone even if I'd been run out with a cattle prod. I didn't want to hear people say sweet things about a man most of them, at one time or another, hated for what he printed in the local rag. Sarah didn't like it, I know. She went through it because she had to. I wanted no part of it. People around Highland like to quote the scriptures, but no one has John 8:32 on a tattoo or t-shirt: "Then you shall know the truth, and the truth will set you free." Happens to be one of my favorites, by the way. I hand-carved it into a plaque above my desk, as if to say, "So there, Brother Vandersma." Read it and weep.

For Crystal, I knew the funeral home would be thick with praise and thicker with irony. We may well be redeemed, but attending your own funeral is questionable, or so it seems. Attending your own visitation creates an odd species of discomfort, or so it seems to me.

Anyway, there we sat, five or six of us, the visitation over, waiting for someone to come and roll the body out to the hearse. We were talking about memories, actually, those of us who'd gone with Crystal, who died of a brain aneurism – *boom!* just like that, at forty-nine years old. I'd have to check. Tragic death, but then we all knew – Crystal too, by the way – that had she continued to draw breathe, she would never have done much else, you know? More deaths than you might think are blessed gifts, believe me.

Casey Aardappel remembered the time we started mic'ing pastors, and that kid from the seminary – Josh-something, we couldn't remember – walked off without pulling the clip-on off his lapel and got halfway up the aisle toward the back before the wire jerked him back like a bull terrier, which made him utter a blessing into that mike unlike any other one ever heard in the sanctuary, a barnyard synonym for excrement.

Evelyn Wensink said she'd never forget the way her own boy, at his own wedding, went down right up there in front as if shot dead, his fiancé's hand in his. Had to get him outside to revive him. My wife, Sarah, said she would never forget the time that retired preacher from Sioux Falls fell asleep during offertory and someone had to nudge him awake to deliver the sermon.

You know – those kinds of things. Mildred Brethhower remembered spending whole services counting knotholes in the pine ceiling when she was a girl. Sam TeWinkle said he'd never forget the time the elders had forgotten to pour the wine into the glasses up front, and the whole church went through communion anyway, just as if the wine was actually there.

Don't know if all of that was redeemed humor or not, but walking into the big church is like wandering through a museum for some of us; and there we were, biding our time, waiting for Andy Hibma, who's been the funeral director here for some forty years and is regarded regionally as one of the finest artists of the dead. Even some of us have been surprised at what that man can do. We barely recognize ourselves.

So, in comes Wade ten Kley. It's just about fifteen minutes since the last of the family left, but he was thinking – we discovered – that the visitation went until seven, not six, and he'd come to pay his respects. So he walks into church through the back door, the back door to the fellowship hall, and what he discovers, shockingly, is he is totally all alone with Crystal's remains, which are remains, you know, despite the expensive accoutrements.

We go mute because this scenario is strange, even for us. And, you can bet, it's phenomenally goofy for him. Just he and Crystal, and she's quite dead.

The casket is at rest in the in lordly yellowing shafts of a late afternoon sun through the north window. There she lies, at rest, as they say, an elegant-but-noticeable smile artistically rendered on her face, all alone, not a soul around but the six of us, sitting in a pew totally outside his radar.

He doesn't know what to do. I mean, a visitation isn't really for the body, but for the grieving, an opportunity to say the right thing, to offer a comforting hug to a husband or a wife or a child. But no one is here to greet, save Crystal, who looks great, having come to us so effortlessly.

We weren't surprised in the least when he turned to go – what's there to say, after all? But oddly enough he stood at the east door, waited a minute, then looked out over the parking lot as if a posse might be out there ready to come for him or the body. No one.

I glanced up at the clock above the kitchen door. It was ten to seven.

He stepped back and walked toward the casket, following the lines the Care Assistants had drawn out, just like the on-time well-wishers had, stopped for a moment to look at pictures, then the video, a slide show of Crystal's life, and then read cards on the half-acre of flowers around the casket. Crystal's own green thumb is legendary, her garden always a feature on the "parade of homes."

"Wade and your husband were friends?" Sam asked Crystal. Wade ten Kley sells insurance and real estate; he's the closest Highland has to a politician, something of a self-promoter, the kind of guy who might shake your hand and pee on your foot at the same time – at least that's what people think. Had Wade ten Kley walked into Crystal's family's visitation earlier, most of the mourners might have wondered what was in it for him, you know? "Golf?" Sam asks. "Pheasant hunting?"

Nobody was looking at Crystal because Wade was standing there beside Crystal's body, grabbing more attention from us thereby than he ever got from anyone alive. But when Crystal didn't answer, I was surprised at the silence, so I turned. She was staring, like the rest of us.

"They went to the same church, dummy," Mildred Brethhower said, defensively, "whole life long."

It was thoughtful of Mildred to cover for Crystal, but it didn't wash because you could say that about a ton of folks, some of them mortal enemies, in fact. That's when Crystal opened up the story. "An old boyfriend," Crystal said, matter-of-factly.

"Seriously?" Mildred said.

Not one of us had any idea. She died young, remember. Not many of her friends have arrived up the hill. Most of us are from her parents' generation.

"In college," she volunteered. "We went to different schools, but I mean here, at Highland.

When we'd be home on vacations, you know? – we were a thing."

We didn't quite know what to say. Meanwhile, Wade ten Kley is standing there beside her body in the classic male piety pose in church, one hand clasped over the other solemnly somewhere below the waist, head slightly bowed as if in prayer, which he wasn't.

"A thing?" Mildred asked.

"Okay, more," Crystal told her. "I loved him maybe." "*Maybe*?" Mildred asked.

"Maybe," she said. "We were kids, you know?" "Serious?"

She tipped her shoulders slightly. "That was years ago," she said. "Years and years and years – I'm certainly not holding a candle."

Remember, we don't read between lines because speech up the hill isn't meant to hide what can't be hidden.

"But were you 'a thing,' I mean?" Mildred kept at her.

"Like I said, *maybe*," she told us, then smiled as if the smile was all she needed to say and we needed to know.

Wade looked around again to be absolutely sure there was no one else in the fellowship hall, then stood stock still, listening for some noise from the basement or something, the ringing sound of cups being washed maybe. Perfectly still. I think he might have died right there if Casey had taken to bellowing like he can.

"And after?" Mildred asked. Crystal had two husbands, after all, not at the same time.

"It was over when it was over – trust me," she told us, and we did.

The moment was strange and awkward but sweetly telling. I mean, there we were, a half-dozen of us from up the hill, basically sitting in the back row of the sanctuary, way on the other side of that spacious room the big church put on when fellowship halls were all the rage; and over yonder beneath the streaming rays of a slowly falling western sun, way over on the north side, stood Wade ten Kley in uncharacteristic silence beside the corpse of Crystal Wesselink, his surprising sometimes-squeeze several decades ago long forgotten. I'm liking this.

Look, we've got ears to die for, literally. Every single word comes in surround sound you can focus like a laser when you want to zero in. We had no trouble hearing Wade breathe. I could have told you right then whether or not he had atrial fibrillation – he did. But every last one of us wanted to see him more closely, the eyes being the mirror of the soul, as you say, so we wandered over and stood there around the open casket like a sextet ready to break into "Whispering Hope."

"The truth is, we were through," he said. He started talking to Crystal's body. He did. We loved it. "The truth is, it wasn't just once."

To me, he seemed a little eager to say that, but I'll be the first to admit that there was something about that man I never trusted. In his favor, it wasn't a gotcha' kind of thing – not at all. But it was news he seemed somehow glad to deliver.

Crystal looked authentically surprised. All of that was years ago, when she'd been a kid. But still, what we all knew was that she hadn't been among us long, so watching her was as promising a venture as watching him; and there they were, alone and together with a story no one knew. Doesn't happen often. I'm all ears.

"The truth is, I wanted it to end," Wade told her body. "I know you were starting to think of rings and all that, but I wasn't sure anymore."

"Were you ever?" Crystal said, *our* Crystal, not his, not the body.

"Maybe, but only because marrying you would have been something like coming home, you know? It's like, you're what's always there," he told her, " – my ace in the hole. Familiar, you know, as the café." He looked around. "Not that I slept around, you know, like at college? I didn't. You know me better than most people do – I wasn't that and you know it."

"Then what happened?" Crystal asked him.

Don't ask me to describe what was going on right then because the rest of us were as shocked as the dead could ever be because we don't, as a rule, carry on conversations with people who've not yet come up the hill. Not that I don't think it's possible – it's just not something we do. There are rules, after all. But Crystal Wesselink was somehow talking to Wade ten Kley in a fashion that left the rest of us nonplussed. My word, that was fun!

"Had to do with drinkin'," he told the Crystal in the casket. "One of those kinds of things, you know?" He put his hands up on the coffin's edge again and smiled – actually smiled, as if all of this somehow made sense, good sense. "Wrong place, wrong time," he told her. "I'm not blaming the booze, either – I wasn't out cold or anything. I knew what I was doing."

In his fingers, he took hold of the satin trim, rubbing it lightly. Gave me the shivers.

"You saying you shouldn't have?" Crystal asked him in this ongoing bizarre conversation. "The problem was that I didn't really know that I shouldn't have," he said. "I didn't feel all that guilty, really, and, after all, it happened twice. That was something I didn't tell you." His eyebrows went up. "What I'm saying is, I told you what happened because – and I've thought about this a lot in all those years – because I really wanted it *not* to work, I mean what was between you and me, I mean. I think something in me wanted it over."

"I don't like this," Casey said to the rest of us. "I don't get it."

"I'm saying what he's thinking," Crystal told us. "This is so cool. I know exactly what he's thinking, sort of. Can you do this to anyone?'

"You be careful," Mildred told her, always the mother. "You just be careful here."

"Every last guy I know said I'd be nuts to tell you about what I did," he told her. "'Hey, what happened, happened, you know? She don't have to know.'" He said it as if all his friends were brainless. If one of you had seen him going on and on like that, you would definitely have thought he was somewhere around the bend. There he stood, yakking to a dead woman. "Plenty of guys got a little on the side, you know? Most guys, I think – Gary Scholten –"

"It doesn't matter who else did what," Crystal told him, almost angrily. "We're not talking about other guys."

"I'm not blaming anybody else, either – I'm really not," he told her, and then, quite boldly, "I came to thank you."

"You what?" she said.

"I did – I came to thank you. I mean I wasn't thinking of it when I came in the door, only to say how sorry I was to Roger and the kids, you know, that he lost you so suddenly. But here we are, the two of us, just like up on that bluff above the river when I told you." He backed away for a minute, as if to give her body a better look at himself, I thought. Strange.

"Thank me? For what exactly?" Crystal said, and I honestly thought that for a moment or so she'd lost her divine standing.

"I told you I slept with Janelle because – I didn't know why, really. I didn't have to," he said. "Janelle would have never mentioned it – you were never friends."

"Because you wanted it broken off," she told him. "That's what you said when you came in here – first crack out of the box. You wanted the two of us to be over, you said – that's why you spilled the beans."

Spilled the beans was a little crude for an angel, but I'm hardly one to criticize.

"You had a thing for him, you said," Mildred interrupted. "That was long, long ago, right?" "We were kids," Crystal told her. "I swear."

"Maybe I just wanted it over – that's what I've been thinking," Wade told her. "You did, too, maybe."

"Doesn't matter what I think," she told him. "The fact is, you slept with Janelle – twice, you tell me now – and you decided you needed to tell me back then, you and me up there above the river, on the bank, standing outside your car – what kind was it again?"

"Chevy Luv – the pickup," he said. "There we were, standing out on that bluff, the only time we'd ever gone there because I honestly thought we needed some place we'd never been, and that's what I told you."

"Worst night of my life at that time," she told him. "Absolutely worst night of my life."

Mildred looked at me as if we ought to somehow get our Crystal home.

"You needed time, you said," Wade told her. "I did."

"You said you needed a couple of days and we'd meet again up there, on that bluff. I've been back there a dozen times and every time –"

"You actually go back there?" Crystal said, then looked at us. "I forgot long ago," she said. "But this is really fun."

"You called it," he said. "You're the one who said it was over, and I didn't fight that, I remember."

"He didn't," she told us. And then, "You didn't," she told him.

"But you remember what you said that night, that last night?" he asked her. "I said it was over –"

"But why? You remember why, Crystal?"

"Because you slept with Janelle," she said, matter-of-factly. "Twice, now I hear – thanks for the news, by the way."

"Your sister told you that if I slept with another girl once, I'd do it again and again – that's what you said. 'I can't trust you, not for the rest of my life,' you said, 'because if you did it once, Wade ten Kley,'" he said, mimicking her, and once again taking hold of that edge of that oak casket, the expensive one, " – if I did it once, I was going to do it again and again and again, as if I were to become a kind of serial adulterer – that's what you said, that's what you laid on me up there on the bluff above the river that night."

"Get your hands off my casket," she snapped, and he did.

"What? – you don't remember?" he asked. "Makes sense, I guess, because you forgot your sister's blessed advice yourself, didn't you?" He chuckled in a way that was quite unbecoming. It was a cheap shot, we thought. It was true, but a cheap shot. "What you told me didn't stop you from doing what you claimed I would be doing, time and time again, too. Don't you think that's just a bit ironic?" he asked.

"I don't remember," she told him, not looking at us at all.

"But it stopped me," he said, "and that's all I wanted to tell you today, and I'm sorry it can only be said now, with you there in that coffin, hearing nothing at all. You can't imagine how many times, when I'd see you in church or on the street somewhere – especially these last years – I wanted to tell you, you were flat wrong about me because I never, ever did it again. I'm not what you said I'd be."

She was becoming one of us. I could see it in her eyes, a kind of emotionlessness, which doesn't mean we don't laugh or cry. She was okay with what was going on. Okay.

"I'm sorry," she said somewhat coldly.

"I was wrong in sleeping with Janelle. I shouldn't have done it."

"Well, good," Mildred told him.

"But I just want to say thanks for what you said that night, thanks for laying that on me the way you did because that prediction your sister gave you sat out there like some kind of legal injunction, a promise I swore not to fulfill – and I didn't. I never did it again," he told her. "What you said made me what it is I've become." He put his hands in his pockets, smiled gingerly, shrugged his shoulders. "I've kept myself away," he said, "and, strangely enough, you didn't." He stopped for a moment, looked around a bit as if some appreciative crowd was just now forming to applaud as he left the stage. "I dang well wish you could hear all of this."

"I hear," she said – Crystal, I mean – who seemed just as untouched as he. "I'm listening," she told him. "I hear every word."

"Good," he said. "Thank you for setting a mark for me."

Wade ten Kley reached up to his lips with his fingers and blew her a kiss, which I thought was a bit smart-ass, but what do you expect? – the man is human.

She returned it, which was cute.

He nodded, as if he'd felt that kiss himself, and he turned around, away from the coffin, started back to the door, then stopped again to watch the slide show playing on Crystal's own iPad – pictures of her as little girl on the farm, playing with cats, then as a kid, braces, a mouth full of tin, a high school cheerleader – you know, the usual, one after another chronicling her life, most of it, at least, some significant chapters unaccounted for, just like all our stories.

"I should be here, you know," he said, pointing at the screen where her lifetime pics were flashing. He actually turned back to the coffin and said it, as if the argument wasn't over. "We were talking about getting married, Crystal. I swear it. And you said no. You're the one who broke it off because I couldn't be trusted, you said. I couldn't be trusted. But none of that you remember – is that what you're saying now? That's all kids' play or something? You don't remember what your sister said?"

She didn't say a thing. That's when we all heard the crack of gravel in the parking lot on the other side of the church. "I can't believe you don't remember," he said, then walked to the north door. He looked back at the iPad still flashing pictures. "I should be here, you know," he told her, and then left.

I didn't know exactly what to make of it. I don't think any of us did. "You honestly don't remember?" Mildred asked her.

Crystal nodded. "I do," she said.

Mildred wouldn't let her alone. "Then you just now lied to him?"

Crystal paused, looked back at Mildred. "Did I?" she said, and then looked around the room behind us, corner to corner, and smiled, an authentic smile – we can tell. "Do you call it a lie if what I told him is what he needs to hear?" she asked. "I don't know the rules."

"There are none," I told her.

She got to her feet and walked out of the pew and toward her body. We all went along. Like I said, we were attending her because she was still getting her sea legs. At her own casket, she brushed his fingerprints off the silver with a hanky she pulled out of nowhere, then read a few notes pinned to the flowers, and slowly moved back up the line to the slide show that featured her whole life, watched the pictures flash for just a bit, then picked the iPad up off the table where it stood beside a gorgeous garden portrait of she and Gene. "Wade is right," she said.

"He probably should be here. He changed my life. Once upon a time he broke my heart and changed my life. So should Milt – he should be here, too."

She was talking about the man she left years ago for Gene, biggest scandal in Highland that year, eons ago.

"I've never forgotten what my sister told me when I told her what Wade had done, and I never forgot what he'd said when we were up there on the bluff. I remember it all. I was lying just now," she told us, turning off that iPad.

"Why?" Mildred asked her.

"Because Wade ten Kley doesn't need to know that I remembered. Wade ten Kley sees way too much majesty in his own shadow," she said, with a giggle. "It'll bug him now – the idea I'd forgotten all of that – it'll bug him, and I think that's okay."

I think we were all nonplussed.

"Pretty cagey, sister," Mildred told her.

"What bugs me is how I forgot myself," she said. "I told him what my sister told me that night, but when I got myself in the same spot, I was the one who couldn't hear it."

"No, *wouldn't*," Mildred said.

"*Wouldn't* – yeah, *wouldn't*." She looked sheepish for an angel, but that's not all bad. "Why is that exactly?"

"Because you're human," Mildred told her.

We were there at the west door, the old entry to the church, all six of us. Mildred was out front, her shoulder leaning up against the door.

"That isn't really a problem, is it?" Crystal asked.

"Not any more," Mildred told her, grabbing her arm with her left, the right one on the door. "Good Lord A'mighty, girl, not anymore." She took Crystal's hand as if she were a child, and off we went, marching out of church, six of us or so – maybe more, maybe less, who's counting?

We walked in a ghostly gang toward Main Street, Highland, right in the middle of traffic, what there is of it, middle of the care assistants coming out of the coffee shop, then out of town, slowly, purposefully, and back up the hill. Walked. The whole time, we walked.

It was one of those warm late afternoons, when what seems to be a half-spent sun lays down a gold sidewalk as if at rest, a walkway up to glory.

That's what it was.

THE NIGHT OF A THOUSAND TEARS

We cry. Even redeemed souls shed tears. Here, up the hill, you'll find just as many wet handkerchiefs as you will in town, and probably more these days with fancy tatting. Listen, the redeemed bawl, but then so did our Lord. This is a story of tears.

I'm going to sound like Rod Serling from *The Twilight Zone*, but there's a ton of characters, and I don't know another way of handling this story.

Meet Clarence de Meester, fourth generation farmer, father of four, and a man who nearly lost it all in the 80s when he tried to shoehorn his sons into his pork operation and instead got himself hogtied and swallowed up by his own debt. You know the scowl on the face of the old man in *American Gothic*? Add hefty jowls and that's Clarence, any day or night after he nearly lost it all *and*, by his own reckoning, lost a son, too. Even though he worshipped the Lord on every last Sunday of his life, his anguished soul gave him no reason to smile. Thank God for deathbed confessions.

Now meet Hilbert Jopinga, rural mail carrier, thin, but hardy, a man as indiscriminate with smiles as Clarence was bereft, and a tortured soul who masked his sadness with face-paint grins when he discovered, as did Clarence did his own, that his son was gay.

That's right – *gay*. In this county, the only place one can really use that word is up here among the redeemed, and that's sad. Trust me – today no one would admit that fact more unhesitatingly than Hilbert and Clarence and their wives. They'll walk over and testify, if need be. Both are here, and these days, both are grinning, their burdens lifted. (Sometimes you just can't help a good cliché.)

The two of them, two local fathers, were here that night, singing stoutly in the chorus of tears, and in many ways, the favored soloists.

Evie de Meester, Clarence's wife, was there, too, as was Hilbert's wife, Marcy, both of whom had taken comfort in each other's arms in the wake of the isolation imposed by their sons' scandalous sexual revelations. They met only three, maybe four times, and then behind closed doors because they knew that their being seen together created an image just as offensive, say, as a street-size mural on the Dollar General would have, an image of their two sons, gay and proud and kissing beneath a rainbow.

Both women are here, too, and these days, they're inseparable. Praise God.

And meet also Sam de Meester, who died about a decade ago and whose death was celebrated with a gorgeous hand-sewn quilt, a single square of that massive, football-field testimony to the Black Death that AIDS became. Sam is and was Highland's only AIDS victim, which is not to say that Sam – or Larry Jopinga – were the only gay men, although they may be the only ones un-closeted.

If you're counting, that's five people around the newcomer that night, plus me, plus hundreds of other lookers-on in death-like silence, some sitting, others leaning up against the stones, a wholesome cloud of witnesses on a night, middle of the drought, as hot and clear as a vision.

And there are more.

Central among them was Eugene Thill, who taught art at the college down the road until he entered the stained glass church bell in a juried exhibition in Des Moines, and won, oddly enough, even though Highland people had never seen it before, and when they did, thought it, well, "different." That brightly-colored bell brought him shows and sales and, eventually, a position at the University. Today, you'll find his stained glass in big churches and cathedrals and some casinos, where the pay is better, he used to say, and there are no damned committees (his language). Eugene Thill is perhaps our most famous resident, even though there are farmers all over the yard who accumulated vastly more wealth. Not that it matters up here.

We're already at six major players, and more are right now stepping out of the stones, as if this were some *Field of Dreams*.

Meet number seven, our former pastor, Rafe van Sloten, and eight, Rinnie Thill, who, despite the fact everyone loved her, still fell into the sleep of death secretly hating the Reverend Rafe for crimes yet to be told. You shouldn't think that even Rinnie's loathing kept her from grace – thank Goodness. Hate poisons the system, but, as Jesus said, let him who is without sin chuck the first stone. You'll have to die to gauge the real depth of that sentiment.

Rev. Rafe was a man whose calling it was to rule, or so he believed. Had anyone told him that was true of himself – and some tried – he wouldn't have believed it, and didn't. But then, the only person Rafe van

Sloten never quite understood was Rafe van Sloten. And no, he's not in Hell either. There are more dreadful sins than mistaken identity, even if it's your own.

The story requires a roster. Feel free to glance back if you must. And now the story.

Eugene Thill had a terribly hard time dying, even though some of his stained glass creations offer a vision as heavenly as anything conceived of on earth – that beautiful. Where he got his talents, I don't know, his parents as ordinary as house finches. The man did art, and his sole determination was to bring God praise.

Not long ago, he arranged a tour, post-mortem, and took most of us along, those who wanted to see what he'd arranged. Think of it this way – maybe a thousand silent apparitions sitting in the long, straight pews of cathedrals, all around the country – time and space being negligible – sanctuaries where colors flowed through the air. I swear, those windows are perfectly wonderful, and we're dead: we see visions nightly – shoot, daily. We know beauty when we see it.

Eugene died an oddly tortured man, despite the glory he could create with his own two hands. He died, begging not to. He bawled and bawled and bawled. What's more, he died half a continent away from the landscapes that lumber handsomely behind so many of his brilliant works, something of an orphan, a man without a home. Hence, his wife's livid bitterness.

Which brings us back to the good Reverend. Reverend Rafe was in his final year or two at the church when the request came from a number of thirty-somethings, women mostly, who discovered that the region's most accomplished stained-glass artist had roots right here along the Rock River. Professor Eugene Thill had been retired officially for several years, but it was these folks' idea to honor him at First Church.

Rev. Rafe van Sloten wondered why he'd never thought of such a show himself. There is, after all, that circular window above the balcony, a Passover lamb, perfectly drawn, in a field of grass beneath an eternal sky, a stained-glass window that catches the sun at dusk almost magically and lights up like an oval goblet of satiny, multi-colored pearls. How often hadn't Rafe seen it when alone and wished he could have called folks to worship right then and there? – a gift from Professor Eugene Thill.

Then, one late afternoon, about a month or so before the show was to open, Harry Fridley knocked on the preacher's office door, then dragged him into the sanctuary. No one else around. Harry pointed at

Thill's precious lamb gift. The afternoon sun was already dropping, the edges of each separate section of that window beginning to glow; but what Harry wanted him

to see was unmistakable – two bullet holes just beneath the lamb's ear he'd never seen before. "I know who did it," Harley said, his cap under his arm because they were, after all, in church, "and I know why – and you should know, too, before you go any farther with this whole exhibition bullshit."

A word about Harry. The pizza joint down the road has an entire wall dedicated to him – pictures, jerseys, hoop nets – because in a quarter century of coaching high school basketball, Harry's teams brought home three state championships and trophies sufficient to make people consider raising taxes for a new high school just to display them all.

Reverend Rafe was aghast at the horrifying vandalism, but that Harry would know who did it was believable, Rafe thought, since Harry knew everyone, everyone knew Harry, and therefore, Harry knew everything.

And so the story began to be told. Stay with me – I know I'm taking a century, but then I'm dead.

The kitchen table in the De Meester home-place is sturdy gray Formica, the painting on the wall? – yes, you guessed it – an old bearded man praying over a chunk of bread. There's a silver toaster against the wall, beveled glass salt-and-pepper shakers, the Holy Bible, and a devotional book Clarence and Evie use each night after supper. A flat head tack on the paneling behind the chair where Clarence always sits holds a fly swatter from the local Co-op atop the bank calendar, thick with scenes from the Canadian Rockies. You get the picture.

Video clips from events we didn't attend aren't available, so I can't tell you exactly what happened the night Charles announced his sexual orientation to his parents, but I can guess, and my imagination these days is as sturdy as it is reliable.

I'm sure Evie did most of the talking. Clarence – he admits it – was struck dumb as stone the moment Charles broke the news. Somewhere along the line that night, almost speechless herself, Evie turned detective, because she honestly didn't know what else to say to her son. "When did you know?" she asked, and Charles, who was late-twenties, said, "Long, long ago."

It's a painful scene to go back to, even for us. What we can't forget stings in the telling, stings even more, if that makes sense. It's just that we know now where to find the exits.

His mother is trying hard not to have to use the hanky balled up in her left hand. "Is it something you just now have come to understand?" she asks.

Her husband's face is pink quartzite.

Now, grant Charles his humanity. He's not as evil as many in Highland think, abandoned by God, nor is he the martyr some might make him, persecuted heathenishly by Highland's Philistines hoard. He's human, is what I'm saying. Today not. Then totally. At that moment, he was in tears himself, tears wrung from a kind of joy that it's finally over, the announcement having been made. But he also sees his parents' total incomprehension.

He'd thought about this, figured out a way to tell them. "You remember those pictures people used to have, Mom?" Charles says, dressed as elegantly as you might expect. "They were strange techie-looking things, all wavy and patterned, and you were supposed to stare and stare and stare until finally some image emerged – you had one you got from some retreat, Mom, the one with the face of Christ."

"Don't go there," Clarence told his youngest son. "Don't even say that name."

"I'm just saying, Dad – you know what I'm talking about, a kind of painting or design that contained within it some image you could see only if you looked really closely, only if you stared? –"

"Maybe you're just seeing things," Evie said. "How do you know it's there if you can't even see it?"

"Maybe you stared too damn long," Clarence said.

"When you see it, you can't not see it," he told them, then stood and walked to the counter where his mother had set coffee, decaf.

It's Evie I feel for when I watch the scene unfold. Clarence thinks he knows the whole truth, and he is already, at this moment, beginning a life without his youngest son, who never liked to farm, anyway.

But Evie remembers the labor, the joy, the pinkish baby in her arms for the first time after all that pain, after all those months carrying him, remembers him rustling, his kicks. She's the one listening; Clarence has already made his judgment. So she carries them both, father and son, in her heart.

And Charles knows how being both wife and mother is killing the only woman he's ever loved, which explains why he tries to explain what he can to her.

"There were moments," he says, "there were things I couldn't account for, that I remember long ago – junior high, even grade school."

He fills his cup and stands there at the counter, away from them. "The way guys talk – you know, Dad," he says. "I didn't get my kicks like that – I could play along, but it didn't matter to me like it did to them – you know, what they did to girls."

Clarence looked down at the Formica top of the kitchen table.

"What about Sarah?" she says. "What about Hanna? What about that woman in California?"

"I was trying to fool myself," Charles says.

"Maybe it'll change again," his mother says. "Maybe some other young woman –" She stops because what she saw in his him was rock solid.

"I knew," Charles tells him. There he stands in a tie and a collar with one of those stays in it, perfectly dressed, his sport coat over the chair where he'd been sitting. "Once when I was…" He stops.

"What?" his mother asks. "I want to understand. Tell us – I really want to know. For my sake," she told him, "for your mother's sake – please, tell me."

At that moment, Charles de Meester, Denver, Colorado, who had already entered a relationship with a man – his very last – but who chose not to break that news just then, said something that nailed itself to the great wall protecting Clarence's heart and soul. He told his parents he remembered feeling something for Eugene Thill, when Eugene was his teacher. He remembered wanting Mr. Thill beside him in ways he knew nobody else – no other high school boy – ever did. He looked down into the cup of coffee. "Maybe it's a piece of the puzzle," he told her.

From that day on, Clarence de Meester, Charles's father, simply hated Eugene Thill, not a difficult thing to do since the Thills had moved to Iowa City a decade before, and absolute cheerless hate is conjured more deftly from shadow than from substance.

So now, back to the Reverend Rafe and Harry Fridley up in the balcony staring at a Passover lamb shot through the head. "Okay, Reverend, who do you know's got a gay son?" Harry Fridley asked him. "Think once – how many gay boys have there been in Highland anyway?"

The preacher knew but he wasn't filling in the lines. "What on earth has that to do with the price of eggs?" he asked.

"Are we on the same wave length here, Reverend?" Harry asked. "You got a candidate in mind?"

"I don't know what that has to do with anything at all –"

"How do you think the gay guy got that way?"

Rev. Rafe stammered a little. "I don't get it," he said, and he didn't.

Harry rolled his eyes. "Do I got to spell it out?" "Yes, dang it," the preacher said. "Yes, please do."

Harry pointed up at the window as if he had a piece in his hand. "His old man," he said.

Things were beginning to focus. "Clarence?"

Harry looked up again at the holes in the window, as if to make them more obscene than they were.

"You're telling me old Clarence de Meester took out his rifle and shot holes in that window because his son is gay –"

"Because Eugene Thill –"

Just like that, the spaces filled in. But the Reverend wasn't going to go down without a fight. "Eugene Thill somehow *made* Charles gay? – is that what you're saying, Harry?"

"You're there," Harry told him. "Now you're seeing it, Reverend."

Credit him with this – Reverend Rafe, right then, just about hated Harry Fridley. "How do you know?" he asked.

"All of that came out years ago already, when Clarence's son said he was, you know, queer."

And then this. "He blamed Eugene Thill, who was gay as Tinker Bell." "You know?"

"A ton of people do." "You're serious?"

"Whether or not I am doesn't count much," Harry told him, pointing again up at the window. "There are others who are."

"Clarence de Meester?" Rafe said again. Immediately, he thought of the Catholics who'd handled child abuse by simply looking past it. Charles had to have been still a kid when it happened, if it happened. "You're sure?" he asked Harry. "I mean we're talking really ugly stuff here."

"Reverend," Harry said, "what I know doesn't matter, but there are others –" "More?"

"Charles isn't the only queer around, you know."

"Larry Jopinga, too?"

Harry hunched his shoulders.

"Hibby Jopinga say so?"

"Go ask," Harry said. "For goodness sake, you're the preacher – you're the one who can ask about that personal stuff."

Reverend Rafe will say today, up here, that his great mistake was not to call on Hibby and Marcy Jopinga, sweet people, wonderful church members he really didn't want to hurt by poking around in a story they held in an iron fist.

The good preacher couldn't help but think that the anger amply portrayed in those two blessed wounds in the stained-glass lamb had to be dealt with, but he wasn't interested in a whodunit. He was God's servant, not a gumshoe. He wanted simply to deal with a situation which could far too easily blow up in their faces. That scared him.

So he drove to Iowa City, where he met with Eugene Thill in the man's studio, just the two of them, and explained as deftly as he could what had happened and offered the possibility that perhaps the show could go on, but that it might be better if the artist himself not show up himself, that the honor still would be his, but only at a distance.

He had no idea what to expect from a man he'd met only once or twice; but if you had asked him before he walked into that studio, he would have bet on anger, even rage, and certainly defensiveness. Rev. Rafe van Sloten would have said – and he admits as much today – that he believed Harry Fridley, not because he had so much respect for the old coach, but because he knew and feared Clarence de Meester. I was there (one night up here) when the Reverend told Clarence, and when he did, old Clarence had to reach for the handkerchief his wife passed him. Such is life up the hill. Wonders never cease.

The thing is, Clarence never took his .22 to town back then, or his 30-30, or anything else from that grand arsenal in his wood shop. He wasn't the one who shot out that Passover lamb, which is not to say he wouldn't have raised holy hell had Eugene Thill come back to town as a sainted hero. No one was happier than Clarence when the whole art thing was scotched.

Eugene Thill sat there on a bar stool in his office, the blueprint for a spacious stained glass creation out before him on the desk, a sprawling map of numbers where colors would go to fit the piece together into a form Reverend Rafe couldn't have made out if he'd tried.

"What are you thinking?" Reverend Rafe asked him, the story now out.

Eugene sat there, moving back and forth slightly on the bar stool, eyes down. "It's not the only show I got," he said softly, then pursed his lips. "Lots of them are bigger," he told the preacher, "but none of them was more important." He looked up.

The preacher definitely heard the word *was*.

"I'm an old man," Thill told him, "and while I've never been at war with Highland or its people. I don't share their politics. I've been away for far too long." He stared across the room at nothing in particular, then looked up once again as if suddenly realizing the preacher was still there.

"A teacher never really knows how any student is going to take what he or she is saying," he told Van Sloten. "I've had students write me and tell me things I don't remember telling them at all – and can't even imagine saying."

The pastor allowed Eugene Thill to talk, allowed him his voice without interruption or even the slightest hint of condemnation, and he never asked whether or not the accusations were true.

"We're mysteries, you and me," Thill told him, placing the palm of his hand down on the blueprint. "We're never quite sure of ourselves, are we?" He looked around the studio as if it was all suddenly foreign. "We're deep, dark holes that cry out for grace – even scream."

That statement, Reverend Rafe thought of as Eugene's own confession of sin.

And with it, the preacher, bless him, snapped the case against him shut.

In two weeks the show was to premiere. Cancellations had to be made. Together in Iowa City, the two of them worked out a plan to say that Eugene had a sudden scheduling problem he couldn't sidestep, that he was laid up with walking pneumonia, and his doctors told him required bed rest. In short, his appearance in Highland was called off, even though some of his works went up – gloriously displayed in digital form, along with a retrospective of his life. All very nice. We all visited.

Quietly and professionally, that Passover lamb was mended by a stained-glass artist in Sioux Falls, Reverend Rafe assuming it wasn't a job he even wanted to offer right then to Eugene Thill.

When Eugene told his wife, Rinnie, she cried in a way he'd never seen her cry before, tears wrung from pain and anger. She couldn't believe how his own people disowned him for a damned lie, and she never once questioned whether or not the accusations could be true. She didn't want to go there, reliving a past when their marriage wasn't a storybook; and she didn't want to go back there, especially now, in retirement, when both of them agreed that things never had been any better.

We're not all-knowing here. I've said that before; you might think of it as a limitation we live with, even though we don't. We're not God or gods, but we're blessed with enough of his grace to be able to say that her tears that day – and that week, and that month – were wrung from emotions that, back then, she herself couldn't have sorted through. She could only stuff her hate into a man she never met, Rev. Rafe van Sloten, who, she reasoned, had buckled under to Highland cavemen. Her husband was an artist, and half of their friends were gay, half at least. She told her husband that if he ever wanted to go back to Highland, he'd have to go alone, which, of course, he did when he came up here after a wearying fight with the Grim Reaper that he still talks about, albeit now with a smile. She couldn't deny him his desire to be buried here, and she was here for the committal; but there was no Highland funeral, not over her dead body, so to speak.

After the preacher died, the two of them, Eugene and Rafe, hugged, but that fateful conversation they'd had in the studio had never been all that rancorous. Up here, when once again the two of them met, it was the preacher whose eyes begged forgiveness, an act which – you won't understand this until you take up residence – is actually as human as drawing breath. Honestly. Just very, very, very hard.

Once she came up the hill herself, it took a month maybe for Rinnie Thill to greet the preacher she'd demonized. Transitions are neither immediate nor, well, total. She knew her husband was looking forward to the homecoming First Church had planned like nothing else scribbled in on a still-active calendar. She would have loved to have seen him adored by the people he grew up with, but because some Neanderthal made a rancid allegation that the gutless preacher swallowed whole, all that joy crashed. And no one had even spoken to her – my word, she thought, if anyone would know whether or not her husband was gay, wouldn't she?

That baggage she carried along up here. But, like I said before, it's all true – burdens *are* lifted.

And now, at long last, we've come to the night of a thousand tears.

If, by grace, I've done this well, then the story needn't go on forever because you're fully capable of imagining at least part of the joy which is to come. You probably know the occasion for that memorable night because all the stories are occasioned by dead people. Who's left? If you've done your work and I've done mine, you know.

That's right, Harry Fridley.

Harry Fridley's demise was as torturous as Eugene Thill's, even more so. We all wish for something sudden – a heart attack, a stroke, a head-on, something that'll grab us by the nape of the neck and usher us nimbly from what is, for you, the here and now. No such luck for Coach Harry. It was positively medieval. I shouldn't be gleeful.

Emergence, like dying, is unique up here. Some folks pop out of new graves as if the earth were a toaster. Some wait a day or a month, some a year – and some never emerge at all. There are choices; we're not automatons. Harry sat still for a time.

No one up here got antsy. Not everything disappears in the twinkling of an eye – well, maybe it does, but adjustment still takes some time, unless you're a child.

Finally, one very, very hot-but-perfectly-clear night, Harry appeared for the first time, rubbing his eyes. He was suited up stiffly in the pinstripe he was buried in but had otherwise never worn.

If anyone is accustomed to crowds, he should be. He's stood before hundreds, huge ones, basketball having been true religion here for three decades, at least. Hesitantly, his eyes still a little smarmy, he surveyed the stones before him. I don't believe he saw any of us, which would not be all that unusual – at that moment, people aren't looking for ghosts.

No one spoke.

Like I said, it was evening. He took a few stutter steps north to check the cornfield just outside the fence, walked even closer so he could see the way the dry, yellow leaves on those ragged stalks were pointing up, arrow-like. He felt, at that moment, *Twilight Zone*-y. No matter how torrid the evening, the recently-arrived know they are not in Hell, but the cemetery doesn't look much like Heaven, either. It's bewildering, and humbling, even purgative.

Who of us speaks first is not something some chief choreographer charts out – we let the Spirit move; and none of us – you'll find this hard to believe – were all that surprised when a woman we'd never seen before stepped out from the crowd, a woman we identified as Sandra Wilkins, who, years ago, was a Meerhof.

And I'm still human enough to know that you need her introduced, even if we didn't. The moment she stepped out we knew the story. You're probably still wondering why Harry Fridley created this elaborate story to keep Eugene Thill – who never once attended a basketball game in his entire adult life – from getting a homecoming. There is more to the story.

Let me say this in an old-fashioned way to suit the parameters of what actually happened. Once upon a time, Sandra Meerhof had allowed Harry Fridley to have his way with her – not just once, either, more often, and for some time, as a matter of fact. Harry was married then, even though he wasn't when he shot out the Passover lamb. As I've said, thank God for deathbed conversions.

Maybe you can guess where this is going. Guilt-stricken, Sandra Meerhof had gone to the person she thought most trustworthy, which wasn't her father, but her art teacher, a man with such a big heart that any serious student who studied with him felt it beat, and she'd told him – Eugene Thill – how what was going on was ripping her up. She knew it was wrong, but she couldn't stop it, just couldn't. It was life, after all, and Harry was so good for her and all of that – you know.

So, years and years ago, this young art teacher from the local college had gone to a slam-dunk high school coach and berated him for what he was doing to a young lady he was killing with his love. That's why she was up here all of a sudden – not so much out of anger, of course, but concern – and I know this word is pushing the envelope – real *angelic* concern. The word is forgiveness. I'm not kidding.

It was the end of yet another scorching day of drought. A remnant south wind, gentle but stirring, ran up the hill and through the white poplars that shade the place, shaking music from the silvery edges of the leaves. It had all the makings of a camp meeting, lots of us there in the semi-darkness – word gets around, after all.

All the main characters were there, too: Clarence and Evie and Charles de Meester, Hilbert and Marcy Jopinga, the Rev. Rafe van Sloten, Rinnie Thill, Eugene Thill, and now this meek little memory, Sandra Meerhof, visiting from some hill in Kansas. We're all there and a hundred others, half a stadium full of redeemed zombies, a portrait of Heaven.

And there stood Harry, alone, facing us, all of us.

Death itself had robbed him of some of his spit and vinegar, but there he stood, this steel nail of a man. He'd been a mover and a shaker, but now, perfectly dead, who should he meet but Sandra Meerhof Wilkins? Must have seemed a bad dream.

I understand what you might like to happen here. I have enough of a human soul to remember what great joy there is in hot blood. I'm sure you're thinking that this woman – forty years or so after her tumble with Harry – would slap him silly, or at least deliver a jeremiad, if not scream bloody murder.

But this is heavenly: she took Harry Fridley in her arms in a way that taught Harry the liar, the adulterer, the winner *and* loser, something profound and other-worldly about grace he'd never thought he needed to understand.

But this story is not about Harry Fridley, a man whose earthly reward is still down the hill in the pizza joint. In that moment, the man was surrounded by a company of folks who might well have skinned him alive, each for reasons not only understandable, but just. Rinnie Thill approached him slowly, reached for his hands separately, took them in her own, and smiled, just smiled.

He was the one who cried.

Our own stained-glass artist had every reason to despise him, every reason in the world. At first, he stood there in front of him like a judge, eyes burning; then he did the strangest thing – he took Brother Harry by the nape of the neck, brought the Coach's forehead to his lips, and kissed him. Harry's face fell into Eugene's shoulder.

Clarence and Evie walked slowly forward. Evie took Harry's hand first, then hugged him quickly. Clarence never once touched him, but offered him the kind of smile he'd lost for most of his life, a smile that was every bit an embrace.

Rev. Rafe van Sloten, who cowered in Harry Fridley's presence and had bought a lie, maybe even for good reason, could barely restrain himself. So he kissed Harry on both cheeks, which I, for one, thought more than a little goofy, but to the point.

Charles de Meester came up, too, gay as a goldfinch, and when he got to the front of the line, the phalanx of forgiveness, Harry reached out for his hand, his arms, his embrace.

All that time – and longer – Harry Fridley cried a thousand wonderful tears, as did we. I don't know that I can say this right, but let me try – it was, for Harry, the finest moment of his life, if that makes sense.

One by one, just as the mourners had greeted his children at the visitation, ordinary folks from up the hill approached Harry Fridley, right there at the edge of the cemetery, at the fence, just beyond that scorched corn field. One by one they welcomed him to their forgiveness, and his own.

Go ahead, tally the anger and list the horrors, but it was a divine reunion that goes beyond my finest words.

The drought-stricken land was bountifully watered that night by a thousand human tears shed from and for the riches of divine grace. It's a story that can be told only in that language, I guess, the language of joyful tears, the only real language we share.

The Lost Sheep

We'd never seen anything close to what happened not long ago when four old folks came up the hill, got out of a big Buick, walked toward the Grevengoed plot, pulled out a non-descript gray box, and proceeded to shake its chalky contents out like fertilizer, even though it wasn't. It was the charred remains of some dear soul.

There those four stood, unsure of how to do what it was they'd been instructed to accomplish. It was Delmar and Erma Braaksma, and her sisters Mary Ruth and Lou Ann, Lou Ann being the only one not a resident of the Pioneer Home. Three Grevengoed sisters.

The ritual came off in slow motion, not simply because all four are old folks, but also because they were skittish about spreading faceless ashes, or handling them, for that matter.

Someone was dead. We had no idea who.

Erma grabbed her husband's arm when that little box was empty because the sisters felt a prayer would be fitting. Whoever was joining us had opted for cremation, and no ceremony, something unheard of. The praying fell to Delmar, the only male.

Before he started, Erma reminded him to remove his cap.

"Lord," he said, chin raised, "into thy hands we commend the spirit of Vivian." Hankies appeared from bosoms. "In your grace, accept her into your kingdom like the lost sheep you so love."

No one knew if the Grevengoeds had another sister. Most of us knew of a lost sheep or two, but not a lost Grevengoed.

"We thank you for the good things she's done," Delmar said. "She loved her cats, and you know she had more than her share of sadness."

We're starting to imagine an image, anyway – a woman heavy like her sisters, same thin hair, round face, button nose, and a shy laugh that makes you think some stern mother had warned her about women who guffawed. Most folks considered the Grevengoeds incapable of iniquity.

"We ask you to forgive her sins, her pride, and her sharp tongue, and that she cared so very little for the fellowship of the saints." The four of them stood there like glacial till, their earnest faces solid granite.

"And forgive us, too, Lord," Lou Ann added. "Remember her for the good works she did with those problem-people she worked with."

They stood freeze-framed until Delmar finally said amen and broke it up.

"It's the way she wanted it done," Erma said. "You read it yourself, Lou."

Their need for ritual wasn't satisfied by a few ashes randomly pitched on dry ground and one impromptu prayer. A life is worth more than that, even the life of a lost sheep. There needed to be more, they silently thought. This Vivian Whoever was gone.

Just then, right before our eyes, the deceased was beginning to show up, rising spirit-like from spent, graying dust, the most ghostly thing I'd ever seen up here – and I live among the dead. She stretched a little, twisted her head as if loosening a stiff neck, stepped back, took an un-la-dylike seat on old Teunis Grevengoed's stone, then sat down jaunty as a crow.

"There's always something new up here," my wife said.

This Vivian was as much a stranger to us as she was to her family. Dark-haired, thin, too, a tad undernourished, more make-up, glasses on a chain – you know, an educated woman. She didn't look Grevengoed.

"What else is to say?" Erma looked around at her sisters. "Still strikes me strange that she wanted to be here." She pointed down the hill toward town. "So *much*, she hated it."

"Must not have," her husband said, "else she would'a stayed in Pittsburgh." "Had a soft spot," Lou Ann said.

"Plain stubbornness," Erma said. "Besides, when it ended, she didn't have nowhere to go." "No man I know would've lived with that woman," Delmar told them. "But several did." Things got quiet. The ladies didn't take kindly to outright smears.

"Time for coffee," he said, looking down at his watch. "What happens now is the Lord's business."

"Still," LouAnn said, "she never had a chance, not with the way she came into things." Maybe she wasn't a sister.

"Awful start," Erma said.

I looked at my wife, who couldn't really put things together, either.

"He'll forgive a whole lot of it, I'm sure – the Lord will," LouAnn said. "You come out of the mess she did, and life's a tough cookie."

"You saying it wasn't her fault – what she became?" Delmar said. "I'm not the one to judge – Jesus is," LouAnn told him.

Delmar got into a snit, said he didn't have to be told that, and off they went, although it took some time before that Buick was headed down the hill and back to town.

And there this Vivian sat aboard the stone of old Teunis.

We tend to let people alone for a time because to find themselves up here is a bit more than most can handle, their minds spinning in mortal cobwebs. People don't believe they'll be just up the hill, but then dying grants generous wisdom that makes the arrival less a shock than you might imagine. You get a whole lot smarter when you die. You'll see.

Nobody laughs, really. Laughing comes later. Lots of people think cemeteries are full of ghosts – well, they are, hundreds of 'em, thousands. And when you find out that's true, you can't help but snicker because it's just sort of right.

My Sarah volunteered to wander over because Vivian looked accomplished, maybe even a little priggish, the kind of woman Sarah likes. Yes, we got favorites. In life, a country editor's wife sees more Pharisees than she does starlings – so many that an honest-to-goodness sinner up here is, for her, something of a dream, pretense totally vanished. Besides, this Vivian needed a woman, is what she didn't have to say. I can still see. I'm not blind.

I don't know where Otto Fredrichson was that afternoon, the genealogist. It would have been helpful to know something more than what little we did right off.

But there she sat on that big Grevengoed stone, staring down into town as if she were about to take out an easel. Sarah walked north along the gravel road down beneath her – I don't know, maybe three rows of stones east, parallel to where Vivian was sitting because you don't just walk up and start talking to a rookie any more than you would to a snowy owl in a bare field. Some folks get scared half to death, so to speak. Sarah wanted this Vivian to see her before she heard her walk up. We really should write a manual.

We could be naked, but imagine the shock. We wear what we choose to, not that anyone has a closet. Think of it this way – a thousand pairs of shoes and not a one doesn't fit. My wife loves it. I shouldn't be making jokes.

Sarah's always been partial to black, and when the two of us got old, anything other seemed sophomoric, so she stuck with it. But she was thinking about how she probably looked deathly to this Vivian woman, so she pulled on a white shawl because she didn't want to seem like something, you know, from Transylvania.

"Pittsburgh?" Sarah said when she came up close.

Vivian had no idea who Sarah was, but she'd been up here long enough to guess that she was, like her, altogether passed on. "I don't know why anyone would choose to live around here," Vivian told her, first crack out of the box – except there was no box. Sorry, I can't help myself. "Something as forsaken as this place might be livable if it weren't for the fecund smells – pooh! How do you live with it?"

"We lead the state in hogs," Sarah said, hitting a deliberately flat note. You got to love her, don't you?

Vivian smiled. "I lived here for a time in my life," she said. And then she giggled, a good sign.

"I just didn't expect to wake up here."

"You were thinking what?" Sarah asked.

"Something more Dante." She raised her hands and shook her fingers excitedly.

"You were expecting Hell?"

"You heard 'em, didn't you?" she said, pointing toward town. "Fire and brimstone?" Sarah asked.

She looked at my wife closely, like a teacher might test a student. "I expected blackness maybe – lights out." Her hands visor-ed her eyes. "You know, in life I could have slapped a dozen comebacks to that 'fire-and-brimstone' line of yours, but I didn't – I didn't even have to bite my tongue." She fiddled with some errant waves of hair, twisting them around her ear. "It's as if I've got a governor in me, keeping the rancor down. That's from dying?"

"It's called redemption," Sarah told her, still trying to be cute. "Redemption?" she said. "You're a preacher, I bet," she said. "Lord, no," Sarah said. "There are no women preachers up here." "In Heaven?" she said.

"In Highland. Heaven may well be full of 'em."

A smile wide as the landscape west spread across Sarah's face – and Vivian's too. That line broke something down.

"Nobody knows you," Sarah told her. "Not that there's a crowd here, but nobody knows who you are."

The smile dropped. "Who are *you* then," she shot back, "if you're not a preacher?" "We just live here is all," my wife said.

"And I'm here, too?" Vivian pushed herself up from the stone and took a step away, west toward the top of the hill. "And there ain't no darkness, and there ain't no fire, huh?" Sarah shook her head smilingly. "You heard 'em – I was always the lost sheep, really was, too."

"Not anymore." "You're serious?"

"Brace yourself," she told her. "This is the new heavens and the new earth."

"This is Highland Cemetery," Vivian said, matter-of-factly, soberly.

"Think of it as a way station," Sarah said. "We're stuck here?"

"You're free to go and travel's a breeze," Sarah told her. "No lines, and nobody tells you to take off your shoes before you go through the scanner."

That made her smile. "No scanner either, I suppose?" "And you don't get stuck on runways."

Her eyes were blue as the June sky, and her hair held the kind of natural wave some women would die for, a cowlick right there on her forehead that swept her bangs back into a tangle of ringlets, gorgeous stuff, the whole mess colored into something bronze, and only slightly unnatural. She looked like an elderly Carol King in a business suit, the kind of woman who would have scared us in life, but then something suggested fear was the frame of mind she'd have wanted us in.

"Takes some getting used to, I bet," Vivian said, "being up here." "Less than you think."

"There are more of you?"

"A whole eternity of us," my wife told her.

Vivian turned around, looking.

"You get this other thing too – invisibility," Sarah said, pointing at thin air. "It's like air conditioning – you wonder how you lived without it."

"And they're all listening?" she asked, sweeping her arm around.

"Divine dispositions aren't given to gossip," my wife said, something of a white lie. "You said you felt it yourself – like some kind of governor in you."

Vivian With-No-Last-Name took a deep breath and let her shoulders sag. "It was that prayer, I bet," she said, "one silly prayer, and *poof!* – I'm here."

Sarah let that alone for the time being, an earthly way of saying it.

Ms. Vivian continued to look around warily. "Is it just you and me talking? Or if I take a swipe here, am I going to smack a bunch of creepy old people?"

Sarah looked around and pointed, as if taking a census. "Some eyes on us right now, and ears. But this is Heaven, you know, or as close as we're going to get 'til glory." She kept her distance. "You'll be fine," Sarah said. "Fear not."

At that point, it seemed to me the woman was getting there – well, getting *here*. In stubborn cases, it might take a day or so, your time. Grace arrives in a moment, but occasionally takes a few minutes to bloom. She brought a hand up to her face as if she sensed an audience. "I never thought I'd be here," she said, "honestly."

"There are lots like you," Sarah told her.

"You don't have to be good to get here?" she asked.

"Some questions don't have answers in language," Sarah said. "You're going to have to determine that one yourself some time, and you got lots of now – *time*, I mean." "You're sure you're not a preacher?" Vivian asked her.

"My husband and I ran the newspaper." Sarah crossed her arms across her chest, shot me a wink, and I materialized, leaned up against Adam Verrips, just a line of graves away. "That's almost on the other side of the divide."

"My old man is here somewhere, I suppose," she said, grudgingly, looking down at the stone. "He's got to be."

"You came for him?" Sarah asked.

She looked up almost angrily. "I had nowhere to go." She shook her head, pulled her fingers up to her lips. "I can't believe I just told you that." She looked around, then giggled. "Besides, I thought they deserved me – I mean, they never wanted a thing to do with me, and now here I am." She looked through the graves around her. "Can I talk to him, too?" she asked. "My father, I mean."

The truth is, we didn't know who her father was.

"His wife is here, too, I suppose – maybe this *is* Hell. For him, anyway." She looked at us closely again as if all of this hadn't made a dent in her doubt. "You're serious about all of what you're saying, aren't you? You're really serious."

"Reach in here," Sarah told her, and with her fingers, my wife reached right into her rib cage. "Grab your heart and feel it – you can do that. I'm not kidding." "Sounds bloody hideous."

"I'm not telling you what to do, but try it – just try it."

Vivian No-Last-Name looked at her right hand, brought it to her chest slowly until it disappeared beneath that business suit. Eyes narrowed. "Still beating," she said. "I can feel it – it's still beating."

"It's just not the one you took home from the factory," Sarah told her, and just like that her hand reappeared.

"A new heart, eh? That's way shocking." She stood up away from that grave, a tall woman. I hadn't noticed the height before. "You know," she said, "seems like yesterday I was in the hospital and this young woman came by, a pastor, the chaplain. I was going in for an operation and it was going to be nip and tuck – I had a brain tumor – and she said her job was to make sure that I felt at peace. 'Make peace?' I asked. 'With whom?' 'With your inner self,' she says, all perfume-y."

Clearly not her cup of tea.

"Young thing – maybe thirty is all. All sweet and nanny-like." She turned around, looked at the stones in the neighborhood again. I liked her. So did Sarah. Maybe that shows.

"So I asked Little Spiritual Girl what her faith tradition was," Vivian said, "and she said she was raised Catholic, but she'd become something else. 'And you're here why?' I asked her. 'To make sure you're at peace,' she told me. "Little Spiritual Thing just smiled, all gorgeous and cute, you know?"

"She's the one who prayed?" Sarah asked. "That chaplain's the one who prayed you here?" "I'm not sure she even believed in prayer," Vivian said, and then she went solid as a statue.

"And who are you, anyway, and why am I telling you all of this?" she said.

"Long-time residents," Sarah told her, pointing to me. "I'm no archangel, if that's what you're thinking."

Vivian pointed to me, then to Sarah, back and forth, back and forth. "We're stuck here?" she asked.

I couldn't help myself – the story was just too good. "She wasn't the one who prayed?" I asked.

"No, no, no," Vivian said. And then, suddenly, "Where is my old man, anyway?"

"It's not like he's got a doorbell," Sarah said. "So who prayed?"

Once things get clearer, they may seem more fogged. She looked at us with what little was left of her earthly self, weighing all of this. That's called doubt, and while some few of us grow out of it quickly, our good Lord has more patience than we ever could muster.

"My mother's not here, is she?" she asked.

Both of us shook our heads, but then we really had no idea who her mother was. Some of the people behind us may well have had some suspicion, but right then, we were on our own.

"I don't know," she said. "Still sounds as bad as that town down there – just some other dimension up here." She pointed down the hill.

"*The mind is its own place,*" Sarah told her, brandishing her English major, "*and in itself can make a Heav'n of Hell, a Hell of Heav'n.*" "Milton," Vivian said.

"What did he know, anyway?" Sarah said. "He was still breathing and stone-blind."

"So what you're saying is I'm sentenced to goodness," she said, "I'm in the good place because of one lousy prayer?"

"I still want to know who prayed," Sarah said. We all did, the others too, wherever they were hanging out.

"So who are you two and why are you here?" she asked, just a bit on the mean side. "I mean, right here, right now, with me?"

What came out was meant to be cute. "We're just a comfort crew, you might say." Sarah told her.

Her eyes narrowed. "Comfort?" she said. "What do you know about me, anyway?"

"My word, we're angels," Sarah told her. Some of the story was coming – I could see it too.

"You were on a ship during the war – something called *Comfort*, right?" "What *don't* you know?" Vivian asked.

We didn't even know there was a Vivian an hour ago. "We don't know your father," Sarah said, but she kept on going with the story. "One of those kamikaze used you to get into Japanese heaven," she said, looking up as if seeing a movie on some invisible screen. "Something like that anyway, right?"

"How do you know that?" Vivian asked.

"A whole bunch of your friends – doctors and GIs, too – dozens, hundreds. Ship goes down, and you were well-marked, right? – all white and a big red cross. Made no difference."

"Hospital ship," Vivian said. "But that's only half the story, really," she said, pointing at her heart actually, pointing almost angrily. "It's not just war that made me *me*. I know what it was like down there," she said, pointing at town, words coming rapid-fire. "I lived here after my mother died – tried to, anyway. My grandparents couldn't handle me, and besides, I don't think they wanted me – they didn't want my mother, either – but then nobody wanted her."

Things were unraveling.

"They were the Christians," she said, still pointing, as if the Buick were right there. "They were the good people, but they turned my mother into a whore, they did." She sat down once again on the man we thought was her father's stone. "And why am I telling you this?" she said. "I spent most of my life listening to people go on and on and on about how bad they had it, and now that I'm dead, I'm the one venting." She pointed to me. "Where did *he* come from?" she asked, "and how many other blessed saints are taking this all in?"

Sarah lifted her finger and drew concentric circles into the air as if to call the heavenly choir to attention, but no one showed because they knew it wasn't time to break into song. "More than you can count," my wife told her.

"You're not kidding, are you?" Vivian said. "You get used to it," Sarah told her.

Vivian looked down at the suit she was wearing, raised her hands, and checked her fingernails as if to document identity. I thought for a moment we were going to be okay. Things were starting to fall into shape.

"I didn't lose faith on the *Comfort*, I just lost friends," she told us, rapid fire, suddenly, like it was something she'd waited forever to get off her chest. "I never had faith, and I shouldn't be here." Some anger maybe, some palpable anger. "For what they did to my mother, I can't forgive them, either," she said, looking over the town. "I wanted my ashes here because I figured it would really piss 'em off. They'd just have to think about me." She brought her hand up to her hair again, as if to primp.

"Be nice if they would," Sarah told her, "but you'll be as gone as the rest of us in a couple of years – more so. Nobody knows you, anyway."

Right then a Chevy van came up the hill and turned into the first driveway just beneath us.

"We got to move?" Vivian asked, getting up.

We told her she'd never see us.

She thought about that for a minute. "Something of a shame really, isn't it?" "It's the way He wants it," I told her. "God?" she asked.

I nodded.

"He's here?"

"He's God," Sarah snapped.

That van rolled to a stop just beneath us. The woman got out and walked over to a grave, a hanky wrapped up tightly in her right hand. She was dressed in a hoodie, a black one, like a monk, a supplicant.

"Her husband died a year ago," I told Vivian. "Maybe twice a week she still comes out." "You all listen in, I suppose?" she asked.

"We hear," Sarah told her. "It's the dead we talk to."

Vivian watched that young woman step out of the Chevy empty-handed, heavy heart. "Here's the story," Vivian said, then stopped. "I can't believe I'm telling you. Maybe you're right – I am different."

It took her forever to get over the hump, but then few of us, I thought, come along so ill-prepared.

"My father was married." She looked down at the Grevengoed grave and spoke, once more, rapid-fire, as if the facts couldn't be reported quickly enough. "And his wife had a baby, and my mother got hired to keep his house clean and his kids in line, food on the table and him satisfied, which, tragically, she did." We had no idea. "Things like that happened, I'm told."

Sarah told her she wasn't wrong. There are others here… you know.

"So my mom got shipped off to an unwed mothers' place in Pittsburgh and never came back here because of the way she'd been treated."

Down the rows of stones that new widow knelt down, and Vivian stopped the speech for a moment. "Doesn't he get to talk to her?"

Sarah looked at me. "I wouldn't say no to that exactly," she said. "So your mother stayed there – in Pittsburgh?"

Vivian nodded. "Nothing for her here." She stood, looked around the stone as if her father would be hiding. "I can't remember all the men, but one of them or another killed her." "Killed her?" I asked.

"Same as." "How old?"

"Way too young."

"Made you an orphan," Sarah said.

And so began her quite temporary odyssey here – with Teunis Grevengoed and his wife and daughters, people, she said, who didn't stand a chance of dealing with her. "There wasn't enough room down there for me," she said, meaning town.

She got into trouble again, didn't say how – and had a choice: reformatory or military. The army sent her to nurses training because the need was so acute, war time, after all. They made her into a nurse, and something else, too, a woman, she said.

"Never dawned on me I'd wake up here," she told us.

And all three of us watched that young woman crowd her husband's grave, put her hands up on the edges of that brand new stone as if she were taking him by the shoulders.

"Must kill him to hear her cry," Vivian said. "Then what?" Sarah asked.

"I ended up teaching, and that's where I stayed for all of my life – nursing, medicine."

The grieving widow got to her knees slowly, then pulled herself up with the help of her husband's new stone.

"That's something I never had," Vivian told me, "that kind of thing. Never."

We weren't surprised.

"Ain't no way I should be here," she told us. "Place like this is for women like that." "Maybe if you did the judging," Sarah told her, and she looked at my wife with what I thought would be the very last bit of fierce human character. "You'd be surprised who's here," Sarah said. "Grumbles and grouches, thieves and drunks, and all kinds of adulterers, not to mention people who worshipped idols."

"Come on," Vivian said. "Seriously," Sarah told her.

For the first time, I saw trust in her eyes, or maybe doubt, depending on your point of view.

"So where is he?" she asked. "Where's my father?"

We still had no idea who he was.

"I wrote him a letter," she said, sitting back on Tuney's stone. "I wrote him because I wanted to know his medical history – I was a nurse. Told him, it was info I wanted to know." "You never heard from him," my wife said.

"So I came here myself, drove all the way back just to see him, and I did." Oddly enough, she smiled. "I caught him coming out of the Co-op. Walked right up to the truck, got right in, told him who I was, and just like that he burst into tears as if he'd expected me on just about every train that ever came back to Highland, Iowa."

All she wanted to know, she said, was medical history; but we knew better. "What'd you say?" Sarah asked her.

"I couldn't cuss him the way I thought I would," she said. "I couldn't. He fell apart. And then he told me he had to bring me home. He said he'd sit down and tell the family. He was an old man. He took my hand and said he was so terribly sorry, and then he told me his wife could never forgive him."

You wonder sometimes how any of us ever make it through.

"He wasn't the mangy bastard I thought I'd meet," she said. "I honestly felt sorry for him – he was gentle and not at all dangerous. I could understand," she said, "my mother."

We could see it hurt to admit all that, but she kept on talking.

"I cried all the way back to Pittsburgh because nothing in my life fit, and I was for believing, like a child, that I could ride in here like some gunslinger, just shoot him up into pieces, set some things square." She pointed at the widow, getting back into her van. "I think it's criminal that he can't talk to her," she said.

"Who's to say he can't?" Sarah told her.

She looked at us strangely.

"How often she come here?"

"Lately, twice a week, maybe – a month ago three, four times. People forget, and that's okay," Sarah told her. "So that's when you changed?" she asked. "You met your father?"

Vivian pointed like a teacher. "What the hell was he thinking when he went into my mother's bedroom eleventy-seven years ago and filled her with his damn passion? She was fourteen years old! And did he ever once think about me? No sir. Never dawned on him that I would end up on a ship holding hands with too many broken and bloody GIs, watch them die in my arms." She stood, but now there was a threat of tears. "And now I'm here," she said, "because of one little prayer."

"Tell me," Sarah said.

"Some nurse who probably shouldn't have done what she did, some nurse came in as I was dying and held my hand the way I'd done so often on that hospital ship, held my hand, and asked – she didn't just do it, she *asked* – whether I'd like her to pray with me – not *for* me, *with* me. That's exactly what she said."

"And you nodded your head?" Sarah asked.

"Never prayed in my life – not officially, you know. But I'd seen enough of death, and I was scared – I'll admit it. I was scared to death of dying. I'd seen a hundred deaths, and you're always alone, finally, when it comes down to it." At the corners of her eyes, I saw something glisten. "I held hands with men and women, kids, like I was, but it doesn't matter, and that's what I knew. When you go, you're alone."

One little prayer.

"One phrase stuck: 'Lord, find Vivian a place with your own people,' that nurse said when she prayed. One little phrase." She grabbed some long grass from the edge of the stone she was sitting on. "It's real, isn't it?" she said, rubbing the blades between her fingers. "I'd never even for an hour of my life been part of 'your people.' Not once. How could I?"

What brought her here, one little prayer.

"I don't know. When I thought about it, I thought of this man who lived here inside his own damned burdens, you know? She never forgave him – did I tell you that? His wife never did forgive him for making me." She looked around once again, nodding as if to make sure she believed what it was she was saying, and where.

"If I had to spend eternity somewhere – what's your name, anyway? I don't even know your name?"

"Sarah," my wife said.

"And if I had to spend my eternal destiny anywhere, I told myself, I could maybe do it with a man who understood how the soul can rot, his own and mine. If he was part of what that nurse was saying – 'your people, Lord' – then I could handle what was coming down the pike, as if I knew. Death, I mean. And then I prayed myself, first time. And last."

When Jacob Grevengoed walked up, we weren't surprised anymore because it was as if he was somehow the one all along, old Teunis's brother. We didn't know him, either, because he wasn't around, really. Honestly, it was as if all of what we'd heard – my wife and I and dozens of others who were praising God and praying themselves right then – as if all of what we heard was exactly what needed to be said to bring Jacob up and out of the grave.

I swear I'd never seen him before – none of us had. And there he was, thin and gaunt and startled as a deer; and she knew him right away, and he knew her because he, too, just then, had learned everything there was to know about her. And none of that could have been done until just right then, I figured. We got ourselves a blessing to be there. We need 'em. Some things don't change.

"Answer me this," Sarah said, later. "Is that woman up here because of two lousy prayers, or because for one moment out of a whole lifetime she believed?" Or is it because, dang it, it's just flat out what He wanted?"

"Does it matter?" I asked.

"Yes," she told me. "Yes, it matters."

"Okay," I told her, "how about this – all of the above."

She took this mammoth breath and let it out like a gusty wind. "Well, that's a heavenly answer, I guess, isn't it?"

And the two of us walked off, leaving the two of them alone in a multitude of smiling faces because I don't have to say what's obvious here: that day there was great rejoicing in Highland Cemetery.

An Intervention for Miss Pris

Pris Vander Wekken took early leave of the vale of tears when ovarian cancer snatched her away from that homey hacienda with the wraparound porch she and Stu built with their own hands on a bluff above the river. She left behind a loving and gentle cattleman, along with three kids, four horses, and a kennel full of princely black labs, not to mention a growing mail-order business in honey, from the bees they kept all over the county. Busy woman, much-beloved.

I sat out her funeral. Bearing witness to so much grief when you know – and this sounds callous – that all the emotion is understandably misplaced is no picnic. Pris's funeral made the Rock River rise an inch or more in salty tears that I had no stomach to watch fall, which doesn't mean I didn't feel it.

After death, you're ready for anything that goes on down the hill. Still, grief can still slay you, even though you know a sweetheart like Pris, with so much to lose, is really going to love her new digs.

But Pris departed when her kids were darlings, barely a sin in sight. So she slugged through their teenage years up here, which wasn't painful, exactly, there being no pain here, but trying nonetheless because she couldn't keep her eyes off what they did or didn't do through those troubling years. Stu is a softie, far more adept at wrestling steers than kids. We're a cloud of witnesses, just as the apostle said, sentries designed to hover implacably, but human enough not to have forgotten the frenzy of what you call "the human experience." We still care. Maybe more than ever. I'm not asking for pity, nor backing a step away from the sheer glory of being redeemed. I'm just being honest, which is not a virtue but a way of life up here.

Pris's first-born, Dylan, fathered a child long before he had any business being where he put himself too regularly in Ang Deters' anatomy. From that undeclared union a child sprang, the first grandchild Miss Pris had, a child subsequently put up for adoption, Ang being just a few months past her sixteenth birthday. Their love child found a home up north with a family named Arends.

Even though Pris would have been smart to stay put along the Rock, this new grandma couldn't, and she didn't; but then, had she not succumbed to death itself, she likely couldn't have stayed out of her first grandbaby's childhood, either. Her angelic status, sadly enough, just made her more adept at hovering. What she saw when that teenager was a kid misbehaving was something she didn't care to go through again and something she'd hadn't experienced in her own earthly mothering, Miss Pris having been – before and after death – Miss Pris.

We have our rules, and intervention is not only frowned upon, it's generally prohibited. But the lure to mess around in our loved ones' lives is that single tree in the garden from which you may not eat – with this unmistakable difference: we can't fall. We're past that.

So we have committees. That'll surprise you, but we do, and one of them rules on Interventions. Even though only a few of us in this place were ever Roman Catholic, someone long ago laid down guidelines that don't differ considerably from the legerdemain of St. Ignatius, who determined, centuries ago, just exactly which mystical visions were legit and which weren't, among mere mortals.

"It's just not the same," Miss Pris edged into the conversation one late fall afternoon. We were having the summer's last glass of iced tea under that statuesque ash in the far northwest corner, the temps a bit over the top, which made the shade as glorious as most things are post-mortem. "It's just not the same," Pris said again, hunching her beleaguered shoulders.

"What's not the same?" Bill Hartog asked.

She doubled down on those hunched shoulders. "It's just different," she said again. "The way they raise their kids nowadays," she told us, "it's just *way* different." She wasn't angry – anger being one of the deadlys, but she was frustrated. You can't blame her, or us. "Maybe we were wrong somehow – you know, the way we did it back then," she said, "but today it's just much, much different – much looser."

"You said it," Bill said.

Most all of us think our kids let their kids get away with too much. Makes us want to scream – angelically speaking.

"I take it something happened," Bill said, because he knew – we all did – there had to be a story.

"What that grandson of mine gets away with," Pris said, eyes flashing, " – it's something of a scandal – no, it *is* a scandal, or maybe a scandal waiting to happen." She'd been up north again.

"He came in late again last weekend after sending a poor young girl right into shock," Pris said, doleful as we'd ever seen her. "I saw it all with my own eyes – he came in late and his parents never even knew, nor did they know have a clue what that boy did and he almost sent a perfectly sweet young girl to emergency. There he was in bed, giggling, then sleeping like a baby, too, yet." She shook her head. "He got away with it – he got away with the whole blame mess." She took a deep breath. "I thought about sitting right there on his dresser and reading him out – 'Grandma from the grave,' like Christmas Past. He doesn't know me. I could have scared the wits out of him, just like he scared the wits out of that poor child – the brat!"

We do use less restrained language, but Pris is Pris. So it all came out slowly, not without some effort.

The Arends named their son Jacob, after his adoptive father's father, the otherwise childless couple a pair of veteran teachers who should have known better than to let that boy have his way as they have. But such is life. Not everything makes sense, neither here nor there.

Jacob was but one of a long line of teenagers to grow up around Lake Havergil, one of dozens to pull off the stunt he did and does, scaring the gee-willikers out of young ladies who should know that jumping into a car full of teenage boys is always a risk. Jacob, who looks like his Marlboro Man grandpa, has little trouble bringing them in.

What Miss Pris watched was a carload of kids in the Arends van going down to the lake just to hear an old story Jacob would tell and thereby scare the uninitiated witless when his headlights flashed over a lane made once and forever crimson, as he would explain, Stephen King-like, with innocent blood. High drama. It was Red Road, Pris told us, an ancient local legend, we'd call "urban," but there's little urbanity up there in the woods.

Look, Jacob was no criminal, just a naughty kid, and, maybe, not even all that naughty.

Mischievous.

But Miss Pris was out of sorts, and when I noticed that undisciplined smirk ripple cross Bill Hartog's tightened lips, I knew that soon enough there'd be a trip to the woods for whoever wanted to board the celestial bus.

Bill himself picked up the story quickly from a platform you might think of as *Wikipedia*, because the bloody dimensions of ye olde legend were made of a horror that Miss Pris, too much a dear, couldn't bring herself to retell. I'm serious – we thought her an angel long before she became one.

'Twas a lover's triangle, Bill Hartog told us – two men, one of them rich, one of them dirt poor – and a woman, the rich man's wife. The rich man owned the poor man, an indentured servant contracted for ten years, maybe more, the details somewhat fluid, changeable, in darkened car interiors, Bill insisted. The poor man kept up the rich man's place on the lake while the rich man did business in The Cities. Something like that.

Now Bill Hartog was, in life, the kind of man who, once upon a time, people waited for at Central Café's coffee time. He's always been a story-a-day guy, blessed with dramatic eyebrows and a register of jokes that, even when he was senile, never quite faded from the cast iron vault implanted in his head. Big talker, fun guy. Could have been a writer but he never had the patience. You know.

The story was legend more than anything, Bill said, and Pris nodded, happy to let him go on, it seemed. It was, he said, part of the lore of the lakeshore that lots of folks up there knew already but loved retelling. Well, most anyway.

The woman seduced the hired man, the poor man – Joseph, enticed by Potiphar's wife, Bill said. He waved his hand in a demure, feminine fashion, a mimicked come-on, as if he were the seductress in some off-the-shoulder gown. Which, to say the least, he's not. A hoot.

"Poor guy dropped his ax beside the woodpile and followed her to her boudoir. You know, same-old, same-old," Bill said. "Who can resist?"

Miss Pris looked teary, but she broke in anyway. "It's Jacob who tells that story, too, adding things here and there, making it worse," she told us. She'd apparently done research on-site. We don't take up much space.

"They breathe new life into the old story line," Bill said, "so something new comes up out of the darkness." Then he flashed a dingy smile – think maybe Jack Nicholson. "Every time they tell the story there's a twist, something new, something to make it come alive. Red Road."

He loved it about as much as poor Miss Pris didn't.

It's almost sacrilegious to say it, but you can't help but giggle at Bill, who's sometimes just a quarter-turn too devilish, but a ball to be around, maybe even especially up here.

All of this Miss Pris had witnessed, and her freckly grandson was the perp. Honestly, it made me want to rent a place up north myself to hear Bill tell it. And it wasn't smart for our sweet Pris to hover around on that lakeshore.

"Moonlit birches leaned into the lake road like a pale tunnel, when Jacob told the story," Bill said, eyes flashing, getting way too much joy out of this, "the only dirt road angling north along the beach, a quarter mile of ruts and bumps off the pavement."

For a moment I thought I was in the car myself.

"Then, one night, the rich man came home and found his wife in bed with the servant," Bill said. "He dragged him outside, tied him to a tree, and hacked the guy to death with the ax," Bill told us, coldly. "Sometimes it's a bayonet, sometimes a hacksaw or a slashing blow from the broken neck of a bottle."

There's no such thing as an R rating up here – we're beyond that.

"Whatever the weapon, the murder happened right there beneath the pines," Bill told us, pointing at that row of Norways just north of us. And then his finger came down, pointing. "You know, uphill slightly from the old barn at the very end of Red Road."

We could have been there. It was Bill holding forth, which was fine with me – Pris nodding, a darling, but no raconteur.

"When Jacob turned off the township road," he told us, "his headlights scattered shadows that sprinted away through the woods, nothing around but trees and an untouched mantle of snow glowing in what slivers of moonlight glanced through the naked branches."

He thinks he's a writer, dang it. He was charming everybody, except Pris, who seemed ready to bawl.

"So the rich man tied the poor man to that tree," he said, "or so the story goes, then slashed at him mercilessly until thick red blood flowed down the drive to where it sat in an indolent pool that soaked into the ground so deep that even today, decades later, the road's dark crimson still shows scarlet in the wash of headlights."

I haven't a clue where Bill got "indolent" from. I needed to look away, so I did, out over the fields north, where I spotted some farmer doing harvest work, big lights spread like day over the rows in front of him. It worked. I didn't laugh.

Dang Bill.

And then, "Mostly it's just pine needles on blacktop," he said.

That's the way the story went, the way Jacob told it, so rich with detail that by the time he'd brought the innocents to the end of the road, the murder was replaying in surround sound, the road beneath the sweep of his lights boldly crimson with bloody terror. Sheesh.

The man had all he could do to squelch delight. It was a great story, and we'd listened in reverie, except Miss Pris, who sat there biting her lip in the same heartfelt concern she must have felt when she was in Jacob's van watching her troublesome grandson terrify his marks.

Bill leaned his weight up and off Frank Pettinga's stone and put his arm around Pris, as we all did, a kind of ghastly laying on of hands. She's so dear.

What had stung her so deeply was a demure young lady named Eve, and I'm not making this up, who knew absolutely nothing of local legend, a sweet girl who'd just moved up north with her family, a pure and innocent young darling Jacob and his friends determined to petrify, and did. Poor Eve, just a mile back up the road, left behind the pizza she'd eaten at the meeting of the newspaper staff earlier that evening, as well as most everything else that had gone into her stomach for what seemed the last six weeks.

And shock. That night, little Eve Winterfield didn't sleep well, even when Jacob did. She'd missed school the next day, left off shivering sometime twenty-four hours later, most of which her parents, like Jacob's, never really noticed.

Pris obviously did, and that's what troubled her so greatly, that and the fact that her grandson was growing ever more adept at pulling the shades down over the adoring eyes of his parents. Even when they knew what went on, they didn't discipline. "It's just different," she'd said, grousing as only angels can.

"There's still some light," Bill said. "What say we head up north?"

So we did.

The Intervention Committee gave us a unanimous nod, since the objective wasn't epoch-making, wouldn't trigger another world war or even a family feud, and there was no death involved. Occasionally, sentries become guardian angels, but only after the IC has allowed a passing grade to a comprehensive plan of action. Think of it as a grant proposal.

The objective, as stated in our prospectus, was clear: young Jacob needed to get his. He'd doled out fear too often and too well, and had never been grounded or even chewed out for his treachery; he even started planning greater unpleasantness. He needed to be stopped at the site of the crime, and who better to smack him down than a gaggle of ghosts arising from the darkened shadows? It was rich.

Pris Vander Wekken is no Joan of Arc. She was not about to lead a band of glorified bushwhackers. She came with, but we could barely get her out of the van.

The plan was simple. Once Jacob's headlights fell over the driveway, a few of us would step out of the barn or wherever and walk slowly toward the car after the fashion that zombies walk out of your multiplex every night these days. We'd throw on some scruffy gear, blotch out our skin to look, well, dead, and become a trashy movie. Great fun, almost scary, your human sense of death so sadly off mark. No matter.

We determined also to make our presence imminently visible only to Jacob, even though Bill suggested creating a flash mob and getting ourselves on YouTube.

Think of us as a goon squad. Vivian came along, the ash queen, a feminist extraordinaire who only, post-mortem, even talks to men; you've met her already. And Billy Brandsma, a builder who took great joy watching blood spurt from the flattened thumbs of his young help; Audley Versteeg, special forces in Vietnam, where, once upon a time, enemy ears hung like mobiles in his jungle shack; and Marcella den Hartog, the quintessential schoolmarm who, had she been Roman Catholic, would likely have left scars on her third-graders, and probably did, anyway. Tough bunch for redeemed dead. I wrote the grant. I went, too. And Bill, the instigator. And demure little Miss Pris.

It was Audley's idea to use the woods, that curving lake road bound on both sides with birch and pine. There was enough cover to play peek-a-boo on the way in, show the kid a few fleeting glimpses of pale and scarred creatures in swaddling clothes, except Audley, who had himself decked out in camo gear circa Sylvester Stallone.

Jacob never saw him or us. That's how deeply he was into the telling.

And let me say it again – this Jacob Arends is seventeen years old and he's not a bad kid. Just naughty – and then, truth be told, not as naughty as some of the angels, me included, and Bill, for sure. Not that we judge.

Still, we love Pris. Vengeance is mine, sayeth the Lord – and we are, for certain, more clearly his servants than you are.

That night Jacob's van didn't hold any innocents. They all knew the tune he was piping, all the rest of them along simply for fun. Once they were close, I climbed in that van myself. It was clear that no one was going to upchuck that night – they were little more than a bunch of three-year-olds begging one more recitation of *Goodnight, Moon*.

The kid, Jacob, was really good – he was really very good.

"Just imagine," he said, *"a thin man with a big fat mustache tied to a tree just outside the cottage, his shirt torn wide open, a rag stretched tight over his eyes and tied in place by a rope around the trunk to pin his head back so tight his neck stuck out when he spoke. His voice sounded scratchy and high.*

"Mr. Franklin," the man yelled, *"don't, please!"*

The kid was, in truth, another Bill; but if there'd been any DNA there, we'd have known.

What you see first is a glint of light from the blade in the rich man's hand: a big man with bright hair falling down to his shoulders. A beard.

Could have used him, part-time, on the Press. I had to laugh when I spotted the rest of the angelic host like wisps of steam appearing and disappearing between the trees. They were having a ball, I'm sure, but they were getting nowhere because Jacob was totally blind to the shenanigans.

"Mr. Franklin," the man screamed. *"I swear. You can't blame me!"*

The bearded man held that big knife at the throat of the servant-guy pinned to the tree, simply held it there, you know? – the bright steel like a mirror.

"Please," the guy screamed. *"Good Lord."* *His wrists were twisted and tied at his chest, you know, as if he was praying or something.*

Not one of those kids was hearing this for the first time. Call it a rehearsal. And wouldn't you know it? – every last cellphone was turned off.

When the bearded man stuck that long knife in him, the servant-guy's legs buckled, and he slumped down, his arms falling to his sides like dead meat.

The intent was discipline: Pris's grandson needed to get stung for throwing Miss Eve into shock, literally, but for a while, in the back seat of that van, almost paralyzed by the spell that kid put on us, I considered adjusting priorities because all of this seemed just too good to pass up. The six of us could add another chapter to the story, a chapter no one in that van would ever, ever forget. We'd become part of the legend's legacy. What we'd do would live on, in other words.

Not that it's a big deal to someone slouching in eternity.

It's hard to explain how long I've been dead, so I won't try, but for a moment there, full of delight, I was sorely tempted to do that which is forbidden.

Pris, the angel, knew it, and in an instant, we were in the bedroom of Eve Maanders, where she was sound asleep. Pris pointed out the stuffed animals, and what came back to all of us was the peace we used to feel when our own children, in booted jammies, were fast asleep in some upstairs bedroom. That joy and peace came back from memories in our own children's rooms. There was Eve, hugging a pillow, a bright blue dolphin beside her.

"He put her into shock," she told us, Pris, Miss Pris. "And he didn't even care."

In the twinkling of an eye, we were back at the bottom of Red Road, Jacob's headlights still twisting through the trees, our mission's objective resolute.

Billy thought it might be a nice touch to raise the hay door upstairs in the barn, then push out those old hay forks and stage a lynching, his, right there at the end of the driveway. That was almost devilish, but I couldn't stifle a grin. Marcella, who missed out on happiness all together until the day she died, quickly pulled a holey feed sack over her head for a mask and played hangman.

Look, I wrote the grant, but I was hardly calling the shots. For a while, it got a little scary, too much of the old man of sin at the edges of what we were up to. The plans threatened to grow wildly out of control. It was just too much fun. Billy tied the rope himself – there was one inside the barn – strung it around his neck, then gave us all one more smile before swinging out over driveway, tongue lolling. It wasn't angelic.

But nobody was looking up just then, nobody. Young Jacob was putting the finishing touches on the story, pointing at the red matting created by pine needles glowing in the van's headlights, the blood never washed from the scene.

I was in the car. I watched. He never once looked up any farther than what he could see before him. Billy squirmed and twisted, as he would have been squirming, strung up there like an assassin. But Jacob was an actor, center stage, his audience eating from his hands, experienced though they were. I thought of grabbing him by the nape of the neck, but we hadn't said anything in the grant about being physical. Poor Billy dangled up there, fun-less. You should have seen him wiggle.

What Jacob couldn't miss, however, was Vivian, the feminist, who, somehow – I honestly don't think she took it with – brandished a handmade machete a yard long, its handle wound with electrical tape. It took an inordinate amount of grace for her simply to lift that thing.

Look. What happened to the woman in the story wasn't part of the plot line. It was the hired man's blood over the driveway, his cries for mercy going unanswered, his death the story. Vivian was doing her own little feminist revisionism here, looking at the whole debacle from the woman's angle – that's what she was up to. And there she was, right smack in the middle of things, her hair – I don't know where she got that wig – cascading in black ringlets around her shoulders like the seductress she never, ever was, a single black strap over her left shoulder barely holding up something she must have grabbed off the rack at Fredericks of Hollywood, thin enough and low enough to – well, you know.

Jacob saw her, this enraged Amazon, and turned to stone. When he did, the others were utterly bamboozled.

"What you see?" one of them said, but the looming female presence flattened him and him alone, although it surprised the heck out of me, too, truth be told.

"What's she doing here?" Jacob said, pointing his finger up over the steering wheel as if it were the barrel of a rifle. "Who is that?"

Of course, no one else in that van saw Ms. Vivian, even though Jacob couldn't miss her – she was standing there like a Superwoman dressed for bed.

"What?" they said. "What you sayin', Jake?"

In her left hand, she brandished that huge blade, but with her right, she waved – how should I say it? – promiscuously, just as Bill had when he told the story. Same thing. A come on, although it looked to me more of an invite to wrestle than to smooch.

Jacob sat there dumb as stone.

And then Audley came up in his fatigues, holding his head under his arm, playing the lover. He stood behind her, square-shouldered, as defiant as someone beheaded can ever be. I can't describe it.

Jacob whispered the kind of language his grandmother didn't know he knew. It came out in a stream of syllables whose profanity wasn't so defined as it was explosive.

"That's the best I ever heard," one of the kids said, the one next to me. "Glory, Jake, you got to do it just like that. If that doesn't curl your hair nothing's going to. We got to get us some women."

Jacob was literally scared stiff.

"Some of us ought to just be here, you know, and when you get here we can come like stalking up out of the darkness," one of them said.

"Cool." "Seriously." "I ain't." "Scared?" "Shit, yes."

On went the dialogue.

"Take a camp stove or something. Call, you know, text…" "What you think, Jake?"

Nothing. Vivian stood there in the bath of headlights, her vague and silver eyes bearing down on poor Jacob Arends.

"Tonight yet?" the guy in the passenger seat said.

"Too late," someone else answered. "We got to wait for some Catechism night or something. There's nobody out now, you know."

"I'm in," somebody else said. "We got this camping lantern, you know. How scary can it be, anyway?"

"What say, Jacob?"

Vivian stood, a Medusa, gray as smoke, snakes for hair.

"Jake?" someone said. "You think?"

Ms. Vivian, whose last name we're still not sure of, was never demure, not in life, or in death, but was showing us a self not one of us, even in death, could have imagined. She took your breath away, really something in a dead person. She'd scaled down her age at least four decades, and was still turning that weapon in her hand, her eyes devoted to Jacob alone. I felt things I hadn't felt so un-righteously for years.

"You okay?" some kid asked Jacob.

I looked around for Pris.

"Who?" Jacob said. That's all.

"*Who* what?" the kid in the passenger said. "What you see, Jakey?"

He pointed over the wheel, shaking his head as if arguing with himself.

"Place gives me the creeps, anyway," one of the kids in the back said. "Let's get out of here."

"I'm all for setting a trap some night, though," the kid beside me said. "Plant a couple of us out here, you know – like lying in wait. Spring it on 'em, you know. *Pow!*" "We could, like, get dressed up," another one said.

"Like the living dead," the kid in the front said. "That'd be great – what say, Jakey? Let's get out of here."

"Zombies," the kid beside me said. "We can video the whole thing, you know? – put it up on Facebook."

Okay, I admit it – I was ashamed.

"Let's go home, Jakey," another kid said. "Let's move."

But the woman before him had frozen Jake's hands to the wheel, ten and two. She held that blade behind her, as if it were suddenly a secret, and came around the van to his door, opened it, and made it very clear, without a gesture, that she wanted him out.

"What you doin', Jake?" the kid beside me asked.

"I'm sick of this – let's get out of here."

When she leaned into that space between the door and naughty little Jacob himself, I realized that, chameleon-like, she'd changed, she'd altered the whole persona, become someone else. She was no longer that woman falling out of her dress, no longer pasty-white, no longer armed; she was, and we knew it because we'd just been in her bedroom, a sweet and innocent teenage girl named Eve Maanders. It was brilliant, really. What Vivian had pulled off was pure genius. There that little girl stood, staring at the boy who'd separated her from her wits – and her supper.

It was Eve Maanders that stared at Jakey just then, Eve Maanders dressed in standard teenage fare – a hooded coat, jeans, bright orange boots that turn down around the ankles, and one of those goofy Sherpa caps with dangly ties. Eve Maanders leaned into the door as if she were right then from the halls of the dead. There she stood a foot away from his face, smiling radiantly, something from another world altogether.

"I don't feel like getting out," some kid said. "Let's get the heck out of here," another said.

"Jakey," the kid beside him said, "what you doin'? Where you goin', anyway?" "It's cold out there – shut the frickin' door, already."

Jake turned almost mechanically, first to the kid sitting in the bucket seat beside him, then a pivot to the rear, where I sat between three others. He stared as if he was suffering a real, honest-to-goodness stroke. He said absolutely nothing, his eyes begging for understanding. He seemed perfectly attuned to where they were right at that moment, to what they were doing, begging them all – each of them – to say something about the sudden appearance of Eve Maanders right there beside him, her face shining pink with life in the warm glow of interior lights, smiling proudly, as if she knew perfectly well that not one of them had a clue she was there.

"Jake, I got a biology test tomorrow," one of them said.

The kid next to me claimed he had to finish an essay for English on Washington Irving.

"You wanting to walk around or what?" another kid asked.

Jake wasn't saying a thing. He turned back to the face of Eve Maanders and somehow realized at that moment that something was being staged here just for him. He pointed at her. "You don't see her?" First words.

The only sound right then was the hum of the engine idle. Maybe an owl. I don't remember.

Nothing but deep-woods silence.

His eyes swung up to hay forks jutting from the loft, where an empty noose swung in the quiet of the lake breeze. I looked around for the crowd. Bill was standing between the pines, arms crossed like Mr. Clean. Aud had backed off, replaced his head, and sat on a stump not far away,

Marcella behind him, all three of them posed like one of those touristy pictures from out west, the OK Corral.

There were three seats in that van, something I didn't realize until Vivian grabbed my shoulder and asked, in a whisper, whether I thought this whole story had gone far enough. That was a surprise, of course, her hand on my shoulder, but not as shocking as the fact that only one of us left, the one outfitted in the garb of the girl who'd been thrown into shock was none other than Miss Pris herself, who stayed at the passenger-side door, her silver eyes glowing on Jacob.

That was shocking.

"I got to get outta' here," he said. "It's time to go." But there she stood beside him, between the car and open door, her face warm with life, no zombie.

Once more, Jacob turned and looked at the others. Once more, he saw nothing but empty faces, and when he did, he perceived as clearly as any mortal kid can that he'd somehow fallen into the middle of something he'd never understand and could never, ever explain. And that look – that cold, dry realization was as close as he'd ever come in his youth to drawing a bead on death itself.

And this is what we know and you don't: that's effective therapy. Trust me.

The girl he knew very well wasn't Eve Maanders leaned in toward him, pulled the straps of that silly cap back with her left hand, and then kissed him, drew back, smiled, and curled her fingers around his cheek, all the while saying absolutely nothing as she pulled the car door shut again behind her and then simply disappeared, taking a place as Pris Vander Wekken behind Vivian and Marcella, two car lengths away, where the whole gang was gathered.

They were all smiling – I swear it. I watched them as Jacob put that van in reverse, checked the rearview mirror, turned that vehicle around as if there was no glow at all on Red Road, and left slowly up the rutted lake lane through the woods.

"What happened, anyways, back there?" one of the kids asked.

Jacob still wasn't speaking.

When we got to the blacktop, I figured it was time for me to head back and clean up behind us.

Then, as if it had never happened, all of us were back at the cemetery, right there beneath that statuesque old ash, all except Pris, who still is prone to hover.

Here's the thing. She was the one who brought the whole thing up, she was the one whose sensitivities were so acute that only Bill could emcee the whole story, she was the one who choreographed that quick trip to Eve's bedroom, and she's the one who upstaged Vivian the avenging harlot, and snuck Eve's winter things from the closet to play the central role. Miss Pris pulled the whole thing off single-handedly.

We'd all been used, we said, chuckling, a bunch of wooden-headed Pinocchios in the hands of the master puppeteer.

Who says up here we ain't got fun?

Jacob didn't sleep well, she said, when she finally returned. She wanted to make sure he was okay. He hadn't upchucked, but what he'd experienced was of such magnitude that when he got home, he wandered into his parents' bedroom and told them the whole thing – well, what he could, a confession Miss Pris witnessed, she said, out-grinning us all.

Bill says to her right then that he'd have never guessed he could enjoy getting hoodwinked the way he had. "You had us dead to rights all night long," he told Miss Pris. "I looked at you and I thought I saw a damsel in distress."

"Men," Vivian said, rather too belligerently.

I swear, Bill turned white as a sheet. "You *all* were in on it?" Bill asked, "*All* you women?"

Remarkably, even Marcella grinned.

And then he looked at me – Bill did. "*You* didn't know, Charlie? Tell me you didn't know."

Too many witnesses in that crowd – I couldn't lie. So I just smiled and let the question go. "I'll file the report in the morning," I told 'em all. "It didn't go exactly according to plan," I said, "but then whatever does?"

Some things don't change.

Yet We Can't Not

This is what he's told us, once or twice, in pieces, chunks, in a card game or two or three.

We remember. Our memories, after all, are divine, and we're stupendous at mysteries.

Westkapelle, province of Zeeland, the hamlet in which he was born and reared, sits closer to England than any other point in the Netherlands, and was therefore heavily fortified against an invasion the German occupiers thought would inevitably be coming once a beachhead at Normandy was established and the battle for Antwerp begun. Nazi bunkers had been sprouting like hard, gray toadstools from Westkapelle's spacious North Sea beaches for years already.

On three sides, the village is surrounded by water. It sits on the island of Walcheren, southeast Holland, overlooking the Schelde, a waterway the Allies had to open to bring their troops and supplies onto the European mainland for the march to Berlin.

The Germans weren't wrong. The invasion came ashore at the village of Westkapelle, the place where Lammert de Lange, just a boy, had lived and moved and had his being. But for him, the invasion itself wasn't the story that changed his life.

Lammie left Holland after the war, when there was no farm on the coast of Walcheren to return to, and the relatives who'd come to this country a generation earlier beckoned generously. In every way, Lammie de Lange grew up during the Nazi occupation; and when it ended, he said there was really nothing for him there, anymore, his parents gone, the farm destroyed by a seawater deluge.

During the occupation, the Underground had ways of communicating, ways of getting out the news. People knew who was a safe bet and who wasn't; and everyone knew the collaborators, neighbors who were often as bad as the SS. There were ways of knowing it was coming, the bombardment, that is, long before it did, and when it did come, no one was surprised.

Lammie was fifteen, young enough to sidestep the conscription so many men from that tiny, isolated, and oh-so-righteous community suffered when the Nazis packed them into trains and dragged them to Germany to work in their factories – no, to *slave* in their factories.

We've got vets galore up here, more and more of the War World II vintage showing up daily, but on those occasions when Lammert de Lange starts into war stories, everything stops, even Rook, and even Izaak de Wild lends a good ear, and Izaak was at Antietam. No one else remembers enemies in the kitchen.

The Underground made sure people in Westkapelle knew, and when the news got out, so did the people. Those who kept their radios had heard the warning from the BBC, and leaflets dropped from the sky the day before, alerting them to the fact Allied bombers would breach the dike that held the water back from fertile land once reclaimed from the sea. The news was a blessing in the form of a warning about inevitable, collateral destruction, but a blessing still, because it gave Westkapelle opportunity to escape, he said, and it suggested longed-for liberation. Listen, in every respect, *liberation* was a word I had to die to understand. Lammie found it much easier, having lived through the Occupation.

The Allies claimed the dike had to go. Not until after the war, he said, had he learned, as many did, that Queen Wilhelmina tried to talk Churchill into not bringing all that destruction to her people and her land, but Churchill listened instead to Eisenhower because the military knew seawater would soften German defenses, making communication and mobility far more difficult – well, more muddied. When the Canadians would finally come ashore at Westkapelle, they could make their way east to Antwerp and meet, thereon, far less opposition.

"Sometimes, maybe, it's better not to know what it is the Queen says." It's just a line Lammie repeats, often with a smirk, when we're playing cards; but for him, that line has roots. Up the hill here, Lammert de Lange is my Rook pal, and, yes, we have Rook – good night, this is Heaven, after all. And when we play, we talk.

What fell first from the sky were leaflets with the word *Waarschuwing* underscored in boldface type – "*evacuatie!*" It was pure joy, Lammie said, because people believed liberation was imminent and the possibility enriched hope. Destruction would descend in the same deafening hours as freedom.

Endless echelons of Allied bombers were nothing new in the gray North Sea skies over Westkapelle; but just a day later, on October 3, some early birds dropped markers, targets, when Lammert was threshing. When he saw them, he took his mother to a nearby farm on higher ground because he'd told her already the day before, when people were already leaving, that they, too, would evacuate once red markers were glowing – Christmas trees, people called them. He'd seen it before, how the Allies operated: first the markers, then the bombing.

He couldn't help thinking, he said, that running away was silly because wherever they would go on foot or horseback there would be other military targets. War was, by 1944, as familiar as the seasons in Westkapelle, but a bloody battle they all knew would come was now imminent.

When the firestorm began, he watched in glee, for which he would not apologize, if apologies were required up here, and they're not. "One of the times, bombs dropped onto the sea dyke and exploded, flinging the bodies of those Germans high into the air," he told us. "I saw arms and legs falling off in mid-air. It was a gruesome sight, but I laughed."

There's no guilt here, hard as that is to believe. You shouldn't think that what he admitted at that moment was confession of sin or testimony – he was not telling us the story as if to defile what we once were, or glory in bliss, now are. Our trespasses are so far behind us as to be forever gone. We tell stories, even stories like this, to explain to ourselves, not just what we were, but what we are, stories that, strangely enough, are really all the same, even though none of them are. No one else here was in Westkapelle.

Lammie's war story has come in pieces that we assemble, even though it's not difficult for him to tell it nor agonizing for us to hear. Really, only when he got here did he put them all together himself. That happens with all of us, and it's a joy, finding some kind of order in what seemed chaos.

Lammert and his mother – his father had been absent for a long time, hiding from the SS – took refuge in a hole in the ground when the British Lancasters appeared, the second wave. There the two of them waited out the bombardment, he says, in a hole in the ground up high enough to avoid the sea water and far enough away from the destruction created by Tallboy bombs opening craters hundreds of meters wide and long.

Hitler himself gave commands that all those bunkers were fortresses meant to be given up only when the last man spent his last shell. Some vets up here were at the Bulge, some at Normandy, and some worked the motor pool all the way to Berlin. But Lammie's story is uniquely his, from the inside, and he was just a kid.

He says he was more afraid than he ever was when it began, shaking in a way he couldn't control, even though he tried, his mother beside him. Even though there were moments when debris showered down like hail, some of that fear eventually subsided. "You can't shake for two whole hours," he told us, even if the ground beneath your feet is waving as if it were a flag, undulating with the relentless concussion.

When he and his mother left that hole in the ground, a handful of Nazi soldiers stumbled by, broken, wandering emptily, as if they had lost any means of determining the direction home.

"In my ears there was nothing but pounding," he said, "but my heart filled with gladness."

English is his second language, not that it makes a difference. We understand.

Lammert de Lange is apple-cheeked, tall, and thin as a poplar. His strawberry hair, dry as straw, simply won't be coddled, so he runs around with rooster tails that make us smile. Salvation doesn't curl your hair or put it into some smooth wave, just in case you harbor such delusions. Lammie is handsome these days only because he is redeemed, as he'll be happy to say. He is here among the beloved, no longer trying to rebuild the dyke that was breached in his heart in 1944.

Nothing in the way he carries himself suggests wounds, but I do wish he'd take the blind more than he does. He's not as competitive as some, not as brave, which suggests that some of us might be cowards or untowardly brash, words that have no meaning now. Still, when the stories come out, we stop shuffling, not because he insists, but because we prefer to listen. If things had been different, Lammie might have been a preacher because most everything he tells us has the moral spin one might expect of someone close to God. We all are, of course, but some of us speak differently, even today.

When finally the bombing relented, as able-bodied as he is, my good friend Lammie was recruited to recover the bodies of a few dozen people – maybe more – from the wreck of a windmill, the place they'd taken refuge when the attack had begun, a place thought strong enough to withstand the assault.

Someday, perhaps, some Brit pilot in a quiet graveyard in Southborough or Berwick-upon-Tweed or Peacehaven will realize that one of the bombs he dropped that night miscarried fatefully, veered away from its intended target, hit a windmill, and killed innocent human beings, men and women and children who, like Lammie, may have been cheering at that very moment – or praying. In a town as religious as Westkapelle, they could have been on their knees thanking the Lord God for bringing the Allies to wrest the jackboot from their throats. To imagine them huddled in prayer at the moment that bomb crashed into the windmill is chilling, and don't think we don't ourselves go zero at the bone, so to speak, at the thought.

A direct hit crushed that sturdy place of refuge, trapping the people inside. Some died instantly, but others lived to experience an even more difficult *deliverance* – and I mean that word in our sense, not yours, although it might be. First there came the bombs, then the resulting flames, then sea water rushing in through the dyke that was no longer there – a crashing sound Lammert says he will never forget, even now. Those poor folks who hadn't died were buried under timbers impossible to push away when the water came. They had no means of escape. Those who weren't killed by the errant bomb or burned in the fiery tumult were drowned in the deluge. Forty-some.

What does he remember? – maybe, we should ask, what is it he will not forget? These things:

The way a couple he knew were found together, pinned beneath a rafter, their little girl, their only child, in the arms of the father, her mother's arms desperately wrapped around her husband; bloated bodies clinging to the walls as if still climbing to escape the rising water; another child, a boy with a harmonica still stuck in his pocket – his mother may have told him to take it along to play while they waited for the end of the bombardment; how unwieldy it was to lift those bloated bodies through the tangled mess that was once a windmill.

All of us up the hill might have returned to Westkapelle when he told the story, might have visited all that suffering ourselves – we can do such things, and we have. We might simply have turned back our clocks and watched the story happen; but Lammert de Lange didn't invite us and would have no part of going back or bringing anyone else back there, either. He tells the story without tears, but not without flinching.

A baby buggy with diapers still neatly stacked inside; pieces of soap to clean up and await liberation; a carpet bag with jewelry and a watch – precious things. A child's piggy bank. Bread. Cheese. And, of course, those dead bodies, some of them floating; and all over, wherever the rescuers walked, thick and sticky mud, brackish sea water everyone knew would choke whatever crops were still in October fields.

Elsewhere, horses stood in water up to their bellies, he says. Animals – wild and domesticated – fled en masse from the flood. Cousins and their children were found dead in a bomb shelter made from reeds and plaster slats.

He doesn't talk about that time very often, and we don't ask because we're not given any more to what amounts to idle speculation. We have no need whatsoever for action movies. But that doesn't mean we don't know stories. We do. It's just they don't weigh us down once we sprout the wings of an angel. I'm not being silly. Death frees you up but good, something you might may want to remember.

Only once have I seen Lammie stagger at the telling – and you shouldn't think the war is an obsession. He would be happy to admit that he spent more time than he should have, more tears, more sleepless nights mulling over that horrible October, both before he left the Netherlands and then even here, the war far behind him. Those days were what he thought about constantly during those long hours when he pulled the rotary hoe or the cultivator, tending his crops on that John Deere that served him so mightily.

Only once did I see him forget the cards in his hand. There was no special reason why the discussion moved in the direction of the war, even though Les Meerfeld and Dirk Visser were there, too, both of them in Europe during that war. It started with the *thwack, thwack* of the medical helicopter that flies out to small-town hospitals to retrieve accident victims or heart attacks, maybe a stroke. It's a troubling sound that stops us from doing whatever we're about because we can't help employing our own little GPS systems the moment we hear it, wondering who and whether or numbers will grow – as they do anyway.

Silence fell, which is not all that unusual up here. That helicopter flew on farther east, its racket falling lower in the register. There we sat at a game. We can and do dream green felt card tables into existence when someone fetches a deck, and the four of us were sitting comfortably beneath that giant maple just west of the bandstand.

It happened at the mill, he said, when, together with a dozen other men, they were pulling the rafters out of the awful mess where bodies still bobbed in seawater. The work was, for a time, hand-to-hand, like a bucket brigade, a couple dozen men and boys at rescue work with no one to rescue. At times, they could and did hitch up the horses to move what couldn't be jerked away by hand; but for the most part, the old Theune Mill was so splintered that getting at bodies jammed hopelessly in the debris was a matter of pulling out shards of wood and tons of rock, piece by soaked piece, field stone by deadly field stone.

They had just removed the body of his cousin, a boy only three years younger than he was, his arm a misshapen mess but bearing no other wounds, which made it likely he had drowned in the rising waters. Lammie was one of a dozen men up the line, when a big chunk of torn wood, a half-door, got passed along, a piece the size of a kid's snow sled, enough anyway for each of them to have to open his arms, he said.

"It was all so fast," he told us. "We worked very hard trying to get at those bodies because we wanted still to believe that we might find someone down there yet breathing, maybe." He poked his glasses up farther on his nose as if to see his cards, but he wasn't thinking about his hand. "This door," he said, gesturing, "it had in white lettering a message, painted on that red barn paint, as if a child maybe took a thin brush, you know, and made the words." He raised his hand as if he were doing the painting himself.

Behind us the strafing sound of that helicopter's blades hadn't yet receded into silence.

He looked up at each of us, eyes sweeping around the table as if he were about to surprise us with good tidings. Then, as if shifting gear, they went into a stare as deep as anything I've seen, a blank, contemplative lapse into bottomless memory.

Time being of little importance, we waited. This part we didn't guess, didn't know. Finally, Dirk said, "No trespassing."

Lammie shook his head.

"'Milk for sale,' I bet," Les said. "Cheese. Cream or something. Fish? – herring maybe."

Lammie smiled at the silliness. He poked a finger in the air as if he were, just then, taking an important call.

"John 3:16," I threw in.

What Lammie was going through inflicted no pain in him. The demure smile that arose from his thin lips held no scorn or dismay, and he seemed not to register our silliness. He was, of course, covering up no brittle anxiety because, hard as it is to imagine, we live now in a world where there is no camouflage.

"There I was, standing with this door in my hands, as wide as my chest," he spread his arms shoulder-width, showing us the cards in his hand, which is not a death-like mistake. Then he looked down at that thing which wasn't in his hands, but once was. "*My only comfort* it said here," and with his pointer finger he drew out the words in the empty air before him. "Right here," he said, and just like that the tattered door appeared like a movie screen in his arms, a chunk of weathered wood wide as the front gate.

All of us understood what was written there, a shibboleth for us and for him, the first line of the answer to the first question of the Catechism all of us knew since we were children.

He rested the bottom edge of the door on the felt, put his cards down, then stood and looked down at what we all saw painted sloppily but clearly across the wood, a little sermon someone in the dark had taken a moment to inscribe while emptying his brush on a door that was now blown apart in the bombardment. *"My only comfort is that I belong to my faithful Savior,"* Lammie said, as if reading the words for the very first time.

You may think of us as children. That's fair. We have this divine sense of knowing where stories will go, like children do, as if we've heard them all time and time again. But great, too, is the joy in the telling, maybe especially those stories that don't get told often or very rarely, if at all, in the scattered darkness which is your world.

We knew that more was coming, knew it in our own hearts, even though none of us had ever removed drowned men and women and children from a windmill in Westkapelle, a place none of us had ever seen. We knew there was more, as a child does, and we longed to hear it all played out.

There Lammert de Lange stood, looking down at *"my only comfort"* like a teacher might point at something important he wanted his students to note on a blackboard, Lammert de Lange, who'd never been anything but a milker. A good one, I might add, but a man who spent his whole life in a barn. There he stood like a prophet, a wise man.

"I held it just for a moment in my hands," he told us, "just for a moment and then on, you know, I gave it up to the next man in line, like all that rubbish we lifted from that mess. But I held it long enough to read what it said, and I told myself," he shook his head as if he couldn't believe it, " – I was just a kid, and there we stood with all those good people dead right behind, uncovered still, something I watched in my mind for the rest of my life – that picture, I mean, of all of us there clearing away the bodies of people who loved the Lord with all their hearts and believed every word of what this means." Then stopped, what seemed mid-sentence. "And I said to myself, what kind of idiot truly believes such nonsense?"

Silence. Again.

But we all smiled. I swear it, we all smiled. Such is life after death.

Me? – I was, in life, in a wheelchair, a victim of polio when I was just a boy, my freedom to roam forever circumscribed once I lost my legs. If you're wondering, it's true – up the hill, I dance. Dirk Visser took shrapnel somewhere between Normandy and the German border and couldn't return to carpentry, the job he missed so badly during his three years as a GI. During the war, Les Meerfeld never made it out of an office, but lost a brother in Korea, and a wife to ovarian cancer.

No one has Lammie's stories, but we all knew that what someone had painted on that door, English or Dutch, was meant to offer suffering souls divine comfort, even before the bombardment, even as they anticipated the horror that reigned from the sky in the name of a liberation they had prayed about for years. We weren't there with Lammie, but we all know that comfort, too, because once upon a time each of us up here had also known what it is to feel little more than bleak despair in the chambers of your heart. We were, all of us, human, after all.

No one else can tell Lammie's story, not even me. But everyone up here understands its lament and doubt and sadness, and the fists at the heavens. Every one of us stood at some pit that held in its maw little more than sorrow and death.

For us, rich pleasure rises from such stories in a manner – believe me – you have yet to discover. It's impossible to explain to a human mind – and for that, I apologize. I retell it now because it is real and it is true, and for a saint like me, it's worth trying to tell you, if I may be so bold. I've still got some humanness in me, and I'd like to try.

Once Lammie said it to each of us, to all of us – "what kind of idiot believes such nonsense?" – we all nodded, idiots in so many ways, all of us smiling because we know for sure now what it is to be redeemed.

For some of us, how hard it is to believe. Yet we can't not. Yet we can't not.

Praise be.

AFTERWORD

Not so many years ago, I wanted to see if I could get a couple of sharp pictures of gravestones adorned in long early morning shadows. I headed out to the Doon cemetery, where the graves hug a rolling hill above the Rock River, a setting that offers a cemetery even more wordless gravitas than most already have.

Frederick Manfred, a prolific American novelist, wanted to be buried up there, to watch over the beloved village of his birth, while sitting up close to fields of corn and beans that, even in winter, don't shed their spacious grandeur.

It was cold that morning in January, and I was just looking for an image that would catch the drama of a new sun on an old grave.

That's when I noticed the stone of a woman whose name I recognized immediately, someone whose life I would otherwise have known nothing of if I'd never read Manfred's, *The Secret Place*.

I read that novel when I was 18 years old, and it made me think I'd like to write stories too someday. But *The Secret Place* wasn't all that popular in Doon. Back then, I only partially understood why not. It's taken me most of a lifetime to see that good people from Manfred's own hometown felt used by his writing that story.

After all, some of it at least was true. Even though Jennie Van Engen was forty years in the grave when *The Secret Place* was published, the novel was based, in part, on her sad, short life.

She died way back in 1920, when she was just 21 years old, or so the stone says. Still, the morning I found that stone, it seemed as if I knew her, or at least of her. I couldn't help wondering how many people on the face of the earth, even among her own descendant family, had any inkling of who she was or the dimensions of her tragedy.

"Till we meet again" the stone says, in mossy text.

I stood there beside that grave, sorry that she'd died so young, and sorry too that Fred Manfred, then named Feik Feikema, caught all the rage he did from the town he loved when he was just trying to tell a really good story, part of it her story. But that some people would be enraged at his using her and them, I understood. Their anger wasn't unreasonable.

Eventually, that moment in the cemetery developed into a short story, the story in this volume titled "January Thaw," a story that imagines what might have been happened when Frederick Manfred's mortal coil was returned to the earth in that cemetery just outside of Doon, Iowa, the same one where I literally stumbled upon the stone marker for Jennie Van Engen.

If they both were there in the Doon cemetery – if something of both of them were residents – what might their spirits say so to each other so many years later? That is what I asked myself.

That story was the only one I'd ever written whose texture was anything other than old-fashioned realism – this young woman, quite dead, taking on the venerable old novelist who had just been buried beside her. Jennie Van Engen's spirit has a score to settle.

After "January Thaw" I started to believe more haunting stories were awaiting me in the cemetery where Fred Manfred is buried, a cemetery just up the hill from the town he loved, even if that love went quite unrequited.

There was, and still is, something magical about being there, or really in any graveyard. The morning I bumped into Jennie Van Engen's stone, I couldn't help but be thankful for a story that made that cemetery alive.

This collection of stories is already dedicated to Frederick Manfred and his Doon friend, Harold Aardema, both of them writers, both of them friends.

But I think it only right that here at the very end I should add yet another to the list of those to whom I dedicate this story, a young woman who died in childbirth almost a century ago, a woman otherwise totally forgotten, known only to those few who've read an obscure novel by long-deceased writer who, with her, is buried in a cemetery up a hill above the Rock River.

What folks are saying about this book

"*Up the Hill* offers twelve short stories of a Midwestern town – from the vantage point of those literally in the cemetery 'up the hill.' The stories' engaging narrator is the village's former newspaper editor. In life, he couldn't tell all the truth in the *Weekly* – but now he can. Sometimes funny, and always touching and wise, this is a book to give to all sorts of people for the hopeful vision it offers of life after death – even particularly to give to seniors or to those facing death. 'We're not all-knowing, if you're wondering, but we're blessed with some pretty cagey powers,' the narrator explains of his post-mortem life 'slouching in eternity.' Like Jan Karon's Mitford stories, *Up the Hill* is rich in humanity and hope."

Barbara Lounsberry, author of *Becoming Virginia Woolf* and co-editor of *The Tales We Tell*

"James Calvin Schaap has done the impossible. In *Up the Hill*, he has beautifully crafted a collection of stories written from the grave, and these voices are both humorous, powerfully moving, and scary. They capture the very 'bones' of what it means to be human – to face one's own transience. With irony and grace, this magical collection captures our attempts for both reconciliation and transcendence."

Mary Swander, Poet Laureate of Iowa and co-author of *Farmscape: The Changing Rural Environment* (Ice Cube Press, 2012).

"Up the Hill is a very original and heartwarming collection of tales that invite readers to listen in on the congregation of the dead as they speak from the afterlife. The characters may not exactly be living our idea of heavenly bliss, but you'll believe the narrator when he says, 'You get a whole lot smarter when you die. You'll see.' Every page sparkles with wit and is bathed with empathy and forgiveness."

Jim Heynen, author of *The Fall of Alice K.: A Novel* (Milkweed Editions, 2012), *The One- Room Schoolhouse: Stories about the Boys* (Vintage, 1994), and *The Man Who Kept Cigars in His Cap* (Graywolf, 1986).

"A fine mix of characteristic Schaap grit and wholesomeness, frugality and abundance, colloquialism and wisdom. If you don't read these stories, 'Honestly, you don't know what you're missing.'"

Diane Glancy, author of *Stone Heart: A Novel of Sacajawea* (Overland TP, 2004) and *Pushing the Bear: After the Trail of Tears* (Mariner Books, 1998), and co-author of *Flutie* (Moyer Bell, 1998), quoting from "The Music of the Spheres," one of the stories in *Up the Hill*.

"When people imagine the dead they usually think zombies or angels, mindless corpses or fleshless sprites. In these sharply told folktales, James Calvin Schaap redeems the dead from these clichéd purgatories. In these ghost stories our dearly departed are canny and keen-witted, vivacious and full of life. There is comedy and tragedy here, and a wonderfully accented narrator who has one hell of an eye for what makes Highland Cemetery an interesting heaven-on-earth."

    Samuel Thomas Martin, author of *This Ramshackle Tabernacle* (Breakwater Books Ltd., 2012) and co-author of *A Blessed Snarl* (Breakwater, 2012).

"Jim Schaap's stories go deep into human experience of communal life in small prairie towns. They are intimate, often funny, and sometimes painful. The only way they'd be better is if you had audio or video of him reading them."

    Virginia Stem Owens, author of *And the Trees Clap Their Hands: Faith, Perception, and the New Physics* (Wipf & Stock, 2005) and *If You Do Love Old Men* (Eerdmans, 1990), and co-author of *Praying with Beads: Daily Prayers for the Christian Year* (Eerdmans, 2007).

"Do the dead being dead yet speaketh? They sure do, and beautifully so in James Schaap's very special narrative voice. These are remarkable stories, unique, wise, painfully honest, and funny as – well, heaven."

    Shirley Nelson and **Rudy Nelson**, co-authors of *The Risk of Returning* (Nelson Family Partnership, 2014).

"It's tempting to call these stories 'Our Town in wooden shoes,' but although the cemetery device is similar, the sensibility is all Schaap's own – full of insight (bordering on wisdom) into how life and people really are, but even more full of affection, forgiveness, and grace."

    Daniel Taylor, author of *Letters to My Children: A Father Passes on His Values* (Bog Walk Press, 2010), *In Search of Sacred Places: Looking for Wisdom on Celtic Holy Islands* (Bog Walk, 2005), *Tell Me a Story: The Life-Shaping Power of Our Stories* (Bog Walk, 2001), and *The Myth of Certainty: The Reflective Christian & the Risk of Commitment* (IVP Books, 1999)

www.ingramcontent.com/pod-product-compliance
Lightning Source LLC
Chambersburg PA
CBHW020933090426
42736CB00010B/1126